I'll Give You a Dollar If You Consider This Art

I'll Give You a Dollar If You Consider This Art

Stories, Poems, Comics, and Other Ponderables
Ripped from the Diaries of

TODDY SMITH and **DARREN NUZZO**

Tallfellow®Press
Los Angeles

Published by Tallfellow® Press
9454 Wilshire Blvd.
Beverly Hills, CA 90212

Visit Tallfellow.com
and
illgiveyouadollar.com

ISBN 1-931290-67-9
Printed in the USA
10 9 8 7 6 5 4 3 2 1

Dedicated to everyone at the library who didn't steal our stuff when we stepped out for a smoke.

Preface
by
Darren Nuzzo

You've seen the misattributed quotes romanticizing writing: that sixty-dollar leather-bound notepad at Urban Outfitters with **"write drunk, edit sober"** printed across the cover in **American Typewriter** font — because typewriters take you back to Bukowski and the beatniks, while Times New Roman reminds you of Ms. Prater and the five-paragraph essay. I understand that nostalgia for the sixties sells better than memories of middle school, but — regardless of the font — no bohemian or beatnik ever actually said, "write drunk, edit sober." And despite what teenage girls on Tumblr insist, it wasn't Hemingway either. I'd like to think that America's favorite minimalist had better grammar than that. (With two independent clauses and no coordinating conjunction, he'd probably use a period, not a comma splice.) More to the point, Hemingway wasn't concerned with alcohol and sobriety or with cute quotes about the craft. He was concerned with good writing. But we all know *that* doesn't sell.

Having recently received a degree in English and Writing Practices, I feel obligated to view these idealistic quotes how an astronomer might view an astrologist — with a quick glance and a long scoff. When you spend your parents' money on four years of liberal arts taught at the weed capital of California, it helps with the guilt to believe your fiction is a product of technical writing, literary familiarity, intellectual labor, and academic discipline — fancy phrases that fit well on a resume — not introspection and imagination, things better taught by a bong rip and Matt Groening.

I thought I was putting my degree to use when I replaced day-dreaming with plotting, imagining with constructing, writing with working, and whiskey with wheatgrass. I even gave up the idea of creativity after reading the works of Mihaly Csikszentmihalyi, a Hungarian Psychologist whose name you likely just skimmed over. I replaced that word, creativity, with productivity. I began waking up early and putting on my slacks and dress shoes and going to the library to write. I no longer stayed home and played make believe. Deep down, I knew there was no difference between a thousand words written at a desk in slacks and a thousand words written on a couch in sweats; but I wished there was. I wanted everyone to know that this isn't a hobby, that this isn't always fun, that picking up a pencil can be just as hard as swinging a hammer. I first tried to write this book this way, with this *work hard* mindset as my motor. I stopped looking up to the gods of creativity and asking them for help; instead, I looked down at my human fingers and told them to type. And that's what they did. For the first eighteen months after graduating, I typed. But not for a Moment did I ever actually *write*.

Whether I like to admit it or not, some of my best stories were written as Instagram captions with my dumb twenty-one-year-old thumbs, laying in my bed at eleven in the morning, hungover and undereducated. That's not a fun fact to face; so even now, I only give it a passing glance. I'll reflect on it just enough to learn from it, to learn that art isn't always like a day at the office. Sometimes it's a diary entry in an overpriced notepad from Urban Outfitters. Sometimes it's staying in bed until inspiration pulls you out. Sometimes it's adding a shot of whiskey to your coffee; sometimes it's adding two shots of whiskey to your coffee. Sometimes it's a lengthy Instagram caption, a poorly punctuated tweet, or a Facebook status that only gets three likes. Maybe good writing, some of the time, actually is just a matter of writing drunk, digging deep inside yourself, pulling out what's real and honest, and holding it above your head for the world to see.

But as I age, it feels harder to hold those things up in the air. My arms feel heavier. My pockets look more inviting. And the decision to write our preface and prologue as personal essays makes my pockets look that much warmer. Todd told me that publishing nonfiction feels a lot like posting a nude photo. But even then, we all know our angles. We know that the mirror in the guest bedroom does us the most favors, that the lamp in the corner should be dimmed two clicks, and that the *Oslo* filter adds an inch. Instead, I tell Todd that nonfiction is worse than just a naked photo — it's a photobook of all the pictures you didn't send, it's those experimental shots, the ones you deleted from your phone and then immediately deleted from your deleted folder. I hesitate to frame those photos — hence this preface I drag on to keep you from Todd's prologue, which I'm certain will expose me from every angle. But I can't procrastinate much longer (carpal tunnel and printing costs). So then, I suppose I'll get Todd started. Cameras ready?

It's twenty minutes past noon. I'm still in my sweatpants and haven't brushed my teeth yet. I'm slouching into the couch, the shape of my spine an homage to our ancestors. I'm drinking my emergency wine that I keep inside my spare tire, pushing *No-Drink January* back to February, maybe March or April. I can't see the words that I'm typing. I'm looking up at the popcorn ceiling and finding friends in the textured finish. I can feel the sun calling attention to the stray hairs on my neck that I'm too scared to shave. I know this isn't the prettiest imagery to end an introduction, but it's a start (and a return) to writing honestly.

Prologue
by
Toddy Smith

In 2013, Darren first handed me his diary, calling it his *fiction notepad*, and said, "Can you just double check that everything is fine?" I assumed he meant grammatically and stylistically, so I groaned histrionically, the way one does when they take on a heavy burden or accidently pick up the 16-pound bowling bowl. I sat down on the edge of his bed for what I figured would be a long night of revisions: Sentence fragment! Comma splice! Pompous Marcel Proust reference!

But as I read, things felt different than they normally do when someone shares with you their work. He looked at me like I was a doctor reading over his test results, not like a friend skimming over his art. He was nervous. I read carefully. It would have been a Moment where I — had I a monocle and a beard — put one on and stroke the other. His words were to be ruminated on, each page a well-documented ailment. It was less of a "slightly high blood-pressure" concern, and more of an "allergic to air and water" concern. But isn't that what diaries are for, to explore your wounds? So the pain didn't worry me. What did was the way he convinced himself that his scars were just scrapes. He used humor to hide the truth. He took a bullet hole to the head and made it look like he just slipped on a banana peel.

"I haven't smoked a cigarette in 18 days," he writes in bold, blocky letters. And then four lines down, he continues, his pen strokes looking lighter and looser and rounder: "But once my money's right, I'll get my consistency back."

It made me laugh. But as I read more similar constructions — deep pain patched up with a punchline — it started to make sense what he really meant when he asked me, "Can you just double check that everything is fine?" He wasn't concerned about sentence structure or rhetorical devices. He was concerned with himself. He was referencing the vague *everything* at the center of everyone's life: how's *everything*, is *everything* okay. And his writing didn't have me convinced that it was.

But, even knowing this, I never set down the red pen. I knew the only terms in which we could talk about this was through writing fiction, by pretending that his diary was artistic make-believe, and by pretending that his emotional support was his editor.

We continued to talk about everything in this language — writing and editing. I'd pull out my red pen and circle a sentence, noting, "expand on this," or "explore that": phrases shared by both editors and therapists.

The second time Darren handed me his diary, it wasn't without a trade. In return, I gave him mine. And that's where this collaboration begins, with two people pushing pain under the rug, passing it off as art.

And as life complicated further, as it has a way of doing with age, so did the extent of our fictionalizing. Fiction wasn't a way to write dishonestly, but rather a way to make our truth a bit less worrisome to those reading. I often joke that I'd write nonfiction, but I don't want my parents to worry. And now that fear of someone else worrying about me had its plus one in Darren.

Our small diary entries had to turn into more complex pieces to keep each other at peace. We treated our entries with the delicacy of an art project so our pain, loneliness, angst, and all things human wouldn't be attributed to us, rather to something imaginative and apocryphal. We leaned on comedic crutches hoping you'd mistake our self-hatred for something funny; and we voiced our pain from characters and narrators so you wouldn't hear us crying. Like storytellers as insecure as us, we learned how to hide an honest ballad behind a big band and strobe lights.

Still, this book is truer than not. Similar to how humans draw a heart as an aesthetically symmetrical shape rather than a gross, slimy, blood-pumping organ, we give you our life in a slightly more digestible way — a way that doesn't force one of us to finally confirm, "Dude, everything *isn't* fine."

In our mid-twenties, we decided to put an end to our diary exchange and move onto more traditional ways of finding and fixing ourselves: spending all our money on plane flights to countries we can't locate on a map, visiting college towns that promise the most Tinder potential, and finishing *The Office* for the fourth time like it's a rite of passage.

Still, I've continued to write in my diary every day. I still write about the guilty life of being a professional social-media-person, my struggles with sobriety, and the rewards of alcohol. I still write about the good kisses and the bad relationships, the manic man living in my head, and the splinters in my heart. And I'm sure Darren still writes about the complications of becoming a respected author in the literary world while also being true to his love for all things low-brow. I'm sure he still writes about his sexual fantasy of someone telling him he's smart, and I'm sure he still writes about his eternal loneliness and how he wouldn't trade that solitude for anything in the world. And I'm sure we both still disguise our pain, wrap it up and put a bow on it, so that if we were to exchange diaries one last time, we'd never have to say that we witnessed our best friend's walking of the plank, even though a part of us both knew that the other had already stepped off and was drowning, sinking, suffocating — but playing it cool, not screaming for help, but instead, with a final attempt at levity, yelling, "Polo!" through the dark water.

There's bound to be a flood in everyone's life. That's the way water works. Eventually, it comes. And you'll have a Moment when you have to grab onto something to survive, not necessarily what a survival guide would suggest or what is objectively your best option, but rather that thing your arm reaches for without your brain telling it to. You reach for what will make you happy in a flood, not what will keep you dry. We could have grabbed our surfboards and paddled; instead, we grabbed our pens and paper and wrote about what it's like to drown.

These past two years, we went back to everything we wrote during our diary days, and together we re-created our writings into something sturdy, developed, and full — something we hope you can reach for when the water rises, something that can keep you afloat while giving you a glimpse of what it would feel like to be under the weight of all that water.

Contents

i'll give you a dollar if you consider this art

Drowning

Everyone was there at the beach — from the Bens to the Savannas. Ben
(the type of kid who just *looks* lactose intolerant) played with a Hacky
Sack, counting out loud each successful hit and cursing in creative accor-
dance to Catholicism each time it dropped into the soft sand: *shootballs!*
Savanna was sunbathing a few towels down, mistaking skin cancer for
Vitamin D. The schoolyard antonym of a Ben, she was tough and inde-
pendent and opinionated, the type of girl who loses her virginity reverse
cowgirl to symbolically slight the patriarchy. The other seven hundred
graduating students ranged up and down the *Ben-Savanna Spectrum.*
And far outside those bounds of measurable teenage behavior, I sat alone
with the sand while the class of 2011 turned it into their playground.

On the border of where the sand turned light to dark, soft to hard,
a group of former-football-players-future-bus-boy-applicants bumped a
volleyball around, naturally leading to a game of Everyone Tackle Everyone.
The high school English teachers kicked off their sandals and pretended
not to be high school English teachers. The wind whipped against the
ten-foot waves and blew my necklace — a scrabble piece of the letter
W attached to a string — away from my body. Beach towels tried to be
kites. The clouds and the sun battled back and forth. People wanted it
to be a beach day, but it wasn't. They were all there: Ben with his boring
allure, Savanna with her confidence, the cool kids enjoying their last
Moments with the title, and the teachers with their three-month weekend.

I was there with my flask and a necklace — no offbeat allure, no
confidence, no cool. Just some kid who liked rum. Just some kid who
liked the letter *W.*

It was tradition for students to go to the beach and hang around Tower 2 on the last day of school. I, however, subscribed to my own tradition. And this year, our traditions overlapped. I sat alone and focused on my drinking, waiting for the perfect Moment to perform my annual ritual. I had done this four times prior and knew better than to do it sober. I suppose high school taught me to think twice about being sober. Then a man with jet-black hair hanging just above his eyes came up and sat next to me.

He took pictures of the ocean and the birds and the sky like they were new oceans, new birds, a new sky. His fascination moved past nature. He took interest in my necklace and asked me what the letter *W* stood for. I had never had anyone ask me before, so I was both eager and nervous to pontificate upon an unhealthy obsession with the twenty-third letter of the alphabet. I told him how I liked the way *W* always moved forward, how *W* could be sharp or round, how *W* was undecided on whether it wanted to rise up or sink down. He listened.

Then I looked at his tattooed wrist and asked him what the letter *P* stood for. He went on to tell me how everything that mattered to him started with the letter *P*. His homeland: The Philippines. His passion: photography. His name: Phillip. I told him he should have opted for the letter *F* because all those things sound like they should start with *F*. He chuckled and put his hand on my shoulder. I liked that about him. We passed the rum back and forth. He asked me if I was here to celebrate the last day of school. I said no. Then I explained my tradition to him. He got a kick out of it. Then he stood up and took his final drink from the flask. He handed it back, touched my shoulder again, said, "empty," referring to the flask, and headed off. I asked him where he was going.

"To go get a tattoo of the letter *F*."

Even if he never got the tattoo, it was the most romantic lie I've ever been told.

He moved softly atop the sand in his rollerblades. He drew his knees towards his chest and took carefully huge steps forward, as if he were a giant stepping over oceans. I looked down at my necklace and then gave my chin to the sky and tried to get more out of the flask, but it was empty, just as he said, and just as I knew. But I didn't want to believe it. I tried again. I didn't mind how pathetic it looked. I was past the point of minding any misery I had. I had no ill will toward my discontent.

I'd spent the last four years with these seven hundred kids on the beach and my best friend at that Moment was Phillip. I knew his letter preference and he knew mine. That was plenty.

"Good luck drowning," he yelled back.

Staring at me from inside the lifeguard tower was my older brother, Grant. On a sunny day he'd be standing outside the tower with his shirt off and eyes on the water, ready to save lives for a generous two dollars above minimum wage. Tourists would walk up to him and ask if they could take a picture with him. They'd even touch his abs if they had had enough nine-dollar drinks or were foreign enough to think a guy protecting the lives of sinking strangers was a tourist attraction. But there were no strangers in the water to save that day. His jacket was still on and his ears were covered by a beanie. He smiled at me and mouthed, "Don't do it." He knew I was going to do it: pretend to drown and make him save me. Then he held up his always mustard-less sandwich and pleaded, "I need to eat my lunch. Don't do it."

I stood up, got in an athletic stance, put my empty flask in my back pocket, and took a three-step leadoff from my towel toward the ocean. My brother mouthed, "Don't, dude. It's freezing." Maybe he meant it. I took another small step.

He loses hope in trying to stop me. He takes his jacket off and sets his sandwich back into his cooler. Then he reaches for his fins. I smile and walk back to my towel. He smiles and murmurs a sardonic *thank you.*

The second my butt touches the towel I spring back to my feet and take off.

My feet conquer sandcastles. My panting laughter outcries the seagulls. I don't turn around. The fear of freezing is dismissed by delight. My knees rise higher as the water turns darker. The wind presses into the waves, erecting them like soldiers. I dive in. They crash down. I'm the only one in the water. I put my head down and swim. Once I make it past the break, a part of me wants to keep swimming. A part of me wants to see how far I can go. But I stick to the script. I flip to my back, let my hips drop, my feet sink, and flail my arms in the air calling for a fake savior for the fourth summer in a row.

There are two lifeguards pacing the shoreline waving their buoys in the air. Ben is on his tiptoes as if that'll help him see further; Savanna is on someone's shoulders pointing out to sea as if I were a piece of undiscovered land; the teachers have their ankles in the water as if to say they are here for me. A white truck emerges through the crowd. The door swings open. A lifeguard steps out and climbs on the hood. She yells STAY CALM through a megaphone that distorts any calm qualities she may have in her voice.

And why aren't I calm? I've always been calm out here. Maybe my brother can't save me this time. Huh, my peace with that possibility is rather unnerving. Maybe I'm lonely. Or is that feeling just the residue of listening to too much Bon Iver this morning? Why are misfits so lovable on television? Everyone loves Abed! Whose shoulders is Savanna on? Is Phillip actually going to get the tattoo? How much do tattoos cost? How often must I drown? Maybe I didn't drink enough. Ya, that's it. That's probably it. I'll close my eyes and recapture my buzz. I'll press my back into the ocean, watch my toes rise up, and I'll lay flat on the water like it's a mattress, like I'm a popsicle stick floating along the gutter on a rainy day. I'll look up at the clouds and let my ears undulate in and out of the water. I'll close my eyes and look for calm.

My mind drifts back to childhood. I think about the times my brother would sit on the porch of our parents' house and count down from thirty out loud while I'd run to hide. I'd go to the end of the cul-de-sac and crouch behind the mean neighbor's lemon tree. I would hear my brother's numbers getting closer to zero. The impatience of a kid — the anticipation of the seeking — sped up the countdown. The final five seconds were the *l-m-n-o-p* of the countdown. The mean neighbor would draw up his curtains, open the window, and yell at me in that way mean neighbors do. My brother would find me and lasso me with the yellow Hula-Hoop, and I'd laugh as if I had won the game.

Things are different now. It takes more to speed up the countdown. It's harder to get people off the porch.

The red buoy flops on my chest, "Saddle up, motherfucker."

"My hero," I joke.

"Dude, you're shaking. You good?"

"Phillip drank my booze. Not drunk enough. I'm so cold."

"Just hold on and kick. You know the drill."

I know the drill. But I can't execute. I can't move. I'm freezing.

"I can't," I manage to say through shivers.

My brother treads water until his hips are in the air and he can see over the white caps toward Catalina.

"Okay. This isn't what I'm supposed to do. But there's a set rolling in. Let's just let it hit us. Okay? It's huge though. You good with that? It'll bring us in. Just hold your breath. Try not to drown."

The wave is double overhead. We hold our breath and hold tight to the buoy and suppress all ocean knowledge and survival instincts, and we intentionally let the biggest set of the day crash on top of our heads. We are in the whitewash. It feels like we are in a washing machine.

I come up gasping for air and my brother comes up laughing.

"Wait, who's Phillip?" he asks.

"Some guy who likes the letter *F*."

Diary Entry #121

Worst Chicken fight Partner

Regardless of my unprecedented ability to drown in the shallow end, my parents insisted I play Water Polo my sophomore year of high school. My fear of swimming, water, and the natural combination of the two, pushed me to learn that I could let my uncoordinated, long limbs stumble between the lane lines while I backstroke into a world of my own. I know it's not spiritually progressive to hide in your head while your body just flops through the day like a level 5 Magic Karp, but it's the only thing that keeps me afloat.

haha

Oh, the buoyancy of the brain!

D.N

8

Growing Up Again

I'm starting to care about things like posture.

I'm starting to care about things like the newest updates on Excel.

Lately I've been thinking about ironing my shirts.

Lately I've been thinking about scheduling my haircuts a few weeks in advance.

And now, republicans make more sense to me than they used to.

And now, the people shining their shoes at the airport make more sense to me than they used to.

Also, there's this new thing I do where I wipe my shoes on the doormat before entering my apartment even when it's not raining.

Also, there's this new thing I do where I say the date and time when I leave someone a voicemail.

I drink responsibly now, even when it's appropriate not to.

I eat vegetables now, even the ones that you don't put cheese on.

I dry my hair before I leave the house.

I wait until I see the garage close all the way before I drive away.

I have one of those razors that you don't throw away.

I have one of those cooking pans that has really specific cleaning instructions.

I know freeways. I know the name of the local meteorologist.

I know what the IRS stands for. I know my blood pressure.

I knew this day would come

when I'd save gas receipts in a folder and save Real Estate shows on my DVR.

I knew this day would come

when I'd save my smiles for special occasions and save used Ziploc bags for my vitamins.

I knew this day would come

when I became a boring adult,

so I saved

a tab of acid in my sock drawer next to a yellow bouncy ball and a Talking Heads CD.

I stick out my tongue

and just *that*

is enough to make me feel like a kid

again.

Reunited

I had an imaginary friend when I was four.
He came back when I was twenty-six.

Just How You Do So Many Things

Your wife isn't allergic to cats, so she's at the party, playing board games that pair well with red wine, getting fur on the black leggings she wears under her floral skirt, and you're at home watching a two-hour special about pharaohs on the History Channel, closing your eyes during toothpaste and car-insurance commercials, considering those allergy shots you saw on a poster at the doctor's office ten years ago, trying to remember what a needle feels like, trying to distract yourself from the paranoid thought that maybe your best friend adopted three cats this past month just for this reason, to keep you out, to keep you breathing calmly in bed, to get your wife into his house while you're at your house — what a fantasy — to get her playing one of those board games that's only fun if you're drunk, to get her scared of getting some fur on her black leggings so that maybe she'd take them off and just wear the skirt. And now you're in the medicine cabinet doing the math on just how many antihistamines it would take to make you immune to cat dander without overdosing. You decide on this: three for allergies, a fourth for the fun. You take it with whiskey. But you should have taken it with coffee. You put on your best clothes and grab your car keys and open the door and buckle up and fall asleep for eleven hours; and you never know what time it was when your wife came home. She's gone to work, and her black leggings are in the wash, soaking, now spinning, now drying on the line. And you pick off with your fingers what the machine and what the lint roller couldn't get off, and you feel the fur between your fingers, looking it over like evidence, and you feel a sneeze banging on the tip of your nose; and you hold it in, just how you do so many things.

Things That I'll Tell You

▸ That guy with road rage isn't listening to The Beatles.

▸ Humanity has a really relaxed way of measuring pulp.

▸ The bad parts of history are better at repeating themselves.

▸ Boys, the friend rubbing sunscreen on your back wishes you asked someone else.

▸ If you're the biggest she's ever seen, she's either a virgin or a liar.

▸ The preference of how I like my steak prepared parallels my patience.

▸ The difference between percentages is greatest when regarding milk.

▸ A trampoline is a great way to get to know your neighbors.

▸ Fame offers limitless opportunities to wear sunglasses.

▸ *Rock, Paper, Scissors* really underestimates the rock.

▸ It's easiest to leave your legacy on wet cement.

As Long As

It's January and I haven't had

sex since summer

except with a good friend

who feels bad for me.

Nevertheless, I am happy

just talking

to this large, sweaty woman

on the stiff couch in her crowded living room

with enough space between us for another person to sit

while other people touch and take shots from the same bottle

and go through the obligatory pre-sex performance:

talk small, smile big, touch occasionally, drink always.

And when sex calls

and groups of two go opening doors down the hall

looking for a room with a bed,

I can be happy

just talking

to this large, sweaty woman

on the stiff couch with space between us,

until tomorrow or until next summer or

as long as she'd like,

as long as I live

with a good friend who feels bad for me.

Dedicated Scholar

I recently read about this Dutch man who studied tomatoes for thirty-five years. At first, I thought he was such a dedicated scholar. Then I decided, he was just a really slow learner.

I Guess the Orange Cat

Dad nods to a trash bag he's laid out for me. He wants me to use it like a glove. Like picking up dog shit, he tells me. I look around the house. I consider the broom and the dustpan. Out back the mouse is torn into three pieces. Dad guesses a red-tailed hawk. I guess the orange cat.

A cat. Dad gets a good laugh out of that one. Not a chance, he explains.

It's because of Moments like this, ones that highlight my ignorance to all things outdoors, Dad says I'll be the first dead in an apocalypse. He even writes it down in case I forget. It goes: me, Mom, our dog Murphy, my brother, then Dad. Maybe Dad will sacrifice himself for my brother. He hasn't decided yet. He'll make his decision when report cards come in. It's always tough love, even in hypotheticals.

The mouse is out back waiting for me. It's been ten minutes now. I've recruited gardening gloves. I've put on athletic clothes and double knotted my shoes. Dad looks at me like I've put on a dress. I squint my eyes so I can't make out the details of what's spilling out of the body. Dad stares at the dead thing while he eats his breakfast. Between bites he doodles on his apocalypse paper. Stick figures of the family. Murphy gets a speech bubble: bark, bark.

He points to his drawing of me. Low hanging fruit, he tells me. I pretend I don't know the expression so he has to explain himself. It dilutes the insult. Gives me enough time to spin it into a compliment. I convince myself that my inclination to cower is actually an evolutionary advantage. For instance, the more disgusted I am by this dead mouse, the further I'll be positioning myself from possible disease. You see, in my head I'm quite clever.

Dad tells me to get on with the job.

"It'll build character," he says.

"Calvin and Hobbes," I say.

"Who?" he asks.

I walk outside and hold my breath. Looking at death, a body bag seems trivial. I peel him off the cement and walk him around the side of the house and past the trash and put him in the green bin with the dead leaves and banana peels, and I start breathing again. The gardening gloves go in the brown bin. I'll explain to Mom later. She'll buy a new pair.

I wash my hands in the pool before going inside.

Dad's on his knees scrubbing the blood from the patio with his thumb and the last few sips of his morning water. My brother runs outside having heard the news of a dead thing in our very own backyard. He drops next to Dad and studies the scene.

"Barn owl."

"Could've been," Dad agrees.

My brother pours the last of the water onto the blood. And now his shirt is off and it's a sponge. They stay out there quite some time. They find a way to enjoy themselves. Dad wipes his bloody thumb on my brother's chest. My brother rubs his chest on Dad's back. They can laugh over all of this. Indeed, two worthy finalists.

Inside, I listen and eat the breakfast they've forgotten about.

"Long-tailed weasel, even."

"Could've been," Dad agrees.

"Heck, coyote maybe."

"Didn't even think that one," Dad says. "Heck, could've been."

The boys keep scrubbing. I bring my dish to the sink and do the same. No soap, no sponge. Just water and thumb. I don't look down. I look out the window at the broken hummingbird feeder, cracked and tipped over, and I call out to Dad, doubling down on the orange cat.

Short-term Memory

After your best friend's heart gets broken he/she will return to you like he/she did after a two-week grounding in grade school: a bit subdued, a little different, a little life sucked from their gut, a little smarter, more cautious, more mature, but only briefly, only for a week or two, and then he/she's back, having learned absolutely nothing, ready to raise hell. Thank god.

Watching the End of The World
by Myself Again

She's Great, Just Asleep

I'm dancing, she's crying into a sock; I can imagine how all this might look. Outside it's much different: there's a forest hugging the town, there are four neighborhood ducks, there's a small plaza where someone might smile at you in passing, there is fog and rain and things you can touch.

After three more songs she tires out and falls asleep. I want to kiss her forehead. If I do, she'll punch me in the nose. It's always a passionate debate. *Space and Love.* That's what I'm supposed to give her in times like these. All the space makes the love pretty tough. Dancing doesn't help much either. I hope the ducks are awake, in times like these it's best that they are.

I tear each piece of bread carefully, like a game of Tetris in re-verse. I'm aware of how pedestrian all this must look — a man playing with ducks in his backyard.

"You're not supposed to feed 'em, ya know?" An old shaky voice calls out from a neighboring house that looks more like a barn. "Hurts 'em bad. Stomach stuff. Messes with the stomach."

Silence waters the grass. The ducks like it that way.

A certain duck, duck number four, even rubs up against my ankles at times, but he's shy today, hiding behind a picnic table. The table is propped upright against two old-growth redwoods. You'd hardly know it was a table by the way it's defaced. Between bites of steak I'll shoot an arrow out the kitchen window at it.

You see, every year Maya gets me a toolbox for my birthday. It's adorable how confused she is in regard to the shelf life of tools. And every year she asks me to build something for her — she's also quite confused in regard to how birthdays work. So I'm building her a picnic table, have been for six years. I've put near a hundred arrows into that table. Haven't pulled a single one out. One arrow is even from Maya, from her best day. I know exactly which one it is. It's like that star that looks the same as all the others, not brighter or bigger even, but for some reason you just see it, just that one star.

The old man keeps shouting through the dark with no damn concern for the ducks, "Why do you keep feedin' 'em? I know you know not to feed 'em."

I weather the storm with more silence. Then duck number four (the one who might be so kind to touch the inside of my ankles) emerges from behind the picnic table and inches toward me.

The old man's voice pushes the duck back for good, "The stomach stuff. I've told you. Hurts 'em bad. You hear me?"

The poor ducks having to deal with this old man shoots a sharp pain into my gut.

"And I want my damn bucket back. Nine years you've had my bucket. My finest milking bucket. I saw you running off with it, laughing and skipping with your wife." That bit really makes me laugh. The old man keeps going, "I've seen it all and I've had enough of this duck stuff. You're turning their stomachs rotten."

I drop the last of the bread and reach for another imaginary piece to keep the remaining ducks a second longer. Then they make their way across the grass. I'm empty-handed with nothing at my feet. I'm better off with bread, but only when I'm getting rid of it. The peasant's paradox, I suppose.

I go inside having not had my fill.

I look at the sink. The day's dishes stare at me like a mother. I grunt at them like a child. I clean them thoroughly. Then I clean the entire house. I iron all Maya's clothes and make sure the laces on her shoes are even lengths at both ends. I do the same with my clothes and my shoes because even that may set her off. I turn on the television and make sure the volume is on an even number for when she turns it on tomorrow. I make sure the soap is either full or perfectly halfway full. She doesn't ask me to do this; she never asks for much, she's great like that. Then I head up to look at her forehead some more.

She's always been self-conscious about the way she sleeps: her mouth opening and closing as if drinking raindrops in her sleep, the tired skin under her eyes filling up with fat. I tell her not to worry, that she sleeps like a princess. It's a shame I'm the only one who gets to see how beautiful she looks.

Maya has only left the house ten times since Dr. Trufant suggested we move here a decade ago: three times to stock up on makeup, six times to buy me a toolbox, and once to steal that old man's bucket. Other than that, she stays in the house all day trying not to get set off by things. I try to stay with her as much as I can.

I watch her sleep and watch the room around her. There isn't much more than empty space. Remember, *Love and Space*. So we live in the corners, trying to do the whole space thing. Our bed is in the corner opposite our dresser: four drawers for her, the bottom one for me. Then there is the record player. And in the most noteworthy corner is the bucket. I can hear the old man yelling every time I see that bucket. I can hear Maya, too, only laughing.

In the bucket are a couple thousand crumpled dollars funding the things we want to do before we die. It's covered with bucket list clichés written in white chalk: *New York for New Years, Eiffel Tower, White Water Rafting, Hear Berlin, Without Return Live at The Troubadour*. We used to be the type of people who'd do these things. A revised version — one more fitting for the type of people we are now — would read something like: *hold hands briefly, share a stack of pancakes.* I still toss quarters in. I like the noise it makes when it hits the metal.

I'm not ready for Sunday. In eight hours Maya will wake up, having not changed a bit, and I'll go to the market. I'll ask her if she wants me to pick anything up for her. She'll say, "If the Egg-Guy has eggs, can you get some?" I'm not proud of how much that question irritates me. The Egg-Guy always has eggs; he's the Egg-Guy, according to his cardboard sign and according to him invariably having eggs. I anticipate my overreaction.

Sleep would speed things up. I shut the front door gently.

Outside is much different. My clothes feel looser, lighter, as if they've been soaking wet all day and are starting to dry from the soft breeze of night. My breathing feels cleaner, deeper. There is rain and fog and things you can touch.

There isn't anyone to wave at in the plaza, so I try the bar. There isn't a line at the jukebox. I play one of Maya's songs she used to dance to. Then I get a drink. I meet someone and get another. All the structure gets to me, so I slip off my boots to mess things up a bit. "Blisters," I'll say if anyone asks.

The girl is sweet and fun and fifteen years younger than me — although I wouldn't have discriminated had she been plain and awful and shared the same birth year. I get her to tell me about her day even though she'd rather just drink and receive a few compliments. She had a dentist appointment and she bumped into a parked car and left a note on their windshield and she even tried that one Greek restaurant that just opened up on 5th Street. *It's all very boring stuff* she keeps trying to tell me. Then she points at my wedding ring, "You're married?"

I look at my fingers. I scan them left to right and nod.

She says *me too*, slips her ring up past her long fingernail, onto the bar, and then into her purse. It's a cheap, formulaic gesture, but I like her. I like the way she moves her hands when she talks and touches my knee after the last word of each sentence.

In her purse I notice a book: a biography about cartoonist George Herriman.

"Krazy Kat and Ignatz Mouse," I say.

"What's that?"

I point to the book to help her out. She seems a bit thrown off by how fast we've moved on from the adultery bit.

"Oh no, it's for my Dad. He tells me what to get him for his birthday. He even gives me the money for it, how sad is that?"

"Have you read it?"

"It's for my Dad," she says again.

"You'll have to borrow it from him when he's done. It's really somethin'."

She looks to her right at the other men at the bar. Maybe these men won't talk about books.

I clear my throat and save the conversation with alcohol.

I buy us two shots of the best whiskey you can get with eight dollars. She insists we interlock arms and take them. I am aware of the way this would look, a thirty-six-year old man and a girl young enough to be buying her father a gift with his very own money interlocking arms and taking a shot. I hate everything about the visual in my head. I look at her bare arm and the skin from her wrist to her shoulder and the few freckles rising from her neck. I take off my jacket, stuff it between my boots, and pick up my shot glass. The insides of our elbows touch. I swallow and then cringe at the taste of eight dollars not being enough. I feel guilty about all the elbow touching.

I jam my feet back into my boots and tell her that I've had enough (to drink) and head home.

I take the longer route home, through the plaza. There's no one out tonight, no one to even wave at. I might as well have my hands in my pockets. I try a diner.

It's an old place — the type of place where you order a coffee by raising a hand and saying, *a coffee.* An old man sits at the counter staring down at a fork and knife and an empty plate. I sit down, leaving three empty spaces between us. He grunts and moves another seat over. I make a mental note that four, not three, spaces is the preferred amount of personal space for a baby boomer staring at silverware at midnight.

A woman sits next to me; the man slides another stool over. She pulls out her reading glasses and scans the menu.

She looks to the waitress and orders with an Australian accent, "I'll have the pancakes, please." Her accent doesn't remind me of the pretty beaches of Australia. More like a chronic smoker who couch surfed in Brisbane for a few months. It's a bit off-putting.

"How many?"

"Oh, it's individually?"

"Yep."

"Two."

I nudge her shoulder, assuming that is a welcomed gesture. "Do one."

"They're that big?"

"No, just not that good."

"Actually, I'll do one," she goes to say, but the waitress is already gone.

We talk as she waits for her two pancakes.

It's all great until, "You're married?"

I look at my fingers and play a poor joke.

"It just fits best on this finger."

She laughs, an awful laugh really, but she doesn't leave — I convince myself that this has nothing to do with her waiting on pancakes. I look at her more carefully. Her eyes need more makeup. Her lips need less color and more moisturizer, her forehead looks nothing like Maya's, and her freckles don't do to me what the last girl's did for me.

Her legs are okay. They move nicely as she struggles to get comfortable. In all, she's still a homely woman — objectively even.

"What brings a married man to a diner at midnight?"

"A sleeping wife."

"What good is a tired wife?"

"She's great, just asleep."

She studies my face trying to find my intentions. I order a coffee. I get my coffee. She grabs me by the wrist, it feels like we are hand-cuffed. She stands up, so I follow.

"Skull it. Let's go."

I chug it. She lets go of my wrist without warning. I feel worse off.

She takes me eight blocks off the plaza to an empty arcade where the smell of pee-stained carpet is half-masked by the smell of vacuumed carpet. It looks like the aftermath of a third grader's birthday party. There are fingerprints on all the screens of all the games and all the basket-balls have made their way to just one machine, a staple when it comes to cheating your way to a high score. I want to take a few shots. The rim is decorated in a chain net. The noise it makes is much different than a cotton net. It's a lovely sound. Instead, we play an alligator game, or crocodile; I don't pretend to know the difference. I bend my knees and get my palms in the ready position as she bends down to put in some quarters. Her knees get comfortable on a discolored patch of carpet. Her shorts are tight so it takes her a while to shimmy each coin from her back pocket. The quarters each take a few tries to be read properly by the machine. They keep slipping through the return slot.

The quarters finally do their job, prompting an invasion of plastic green monsters. I stand slightly off from the center of the machine to let her know that I don't mind her joining me. She stays in a squatting position and curls up to my right ankle. I hit each alligator with my palm. She rubs her hands up and down my shins. My leg hair doesn't bother her how it might some. The alligators start coming quicker. I bend my knees some. My quads and hamstrings tighten. My traps fill with blood and rise closer to my ears. All of my hits are now with a closed fist.

I can feel her hands working their way up my shorts. She navigates her fingertips around the inside of my thigh, through the hair on my leg, and plays with the buttons on my briefs.

The game ends; I look around for more quarters.

⏩

I stare at Maya's forehead before heading downstairs to sleep on the couch.

Morning comes and Maya is nothing more than the same. My clothes feel wet, my breathing is flat, and there's just a whole bunch of space, too much to care for.

I'm not in much pain. I suppose when you've been shot nine times the tenth is more a number than a bullet.

Before I head out for the market, I stop at our bedroom door and reach into the bucket, find two twenties and mess around with the change, hoping she'd hear it and make a fuss about how that money is for us and not groceries. She doesn't budge. I walk to the record player and drop the needle: *Berlin, Without Return*.

"I think we should dance."

She doesn't say anything.

"Well, come on."

She keeps with the whole silence bit.

"I really think we should."

She takes off a sock and brings it to her cheek even though she's not crying quite yet.

"Would it hurt you to dance with me?"

Then she points to her socked foot tapping the ground and then nods at my socked foot tapping the ground, insisting that she is dancing with me.

"You're awful. You're miserable and awful."

Now she's really crying.

"Just stand up and let me dance with you."

"I'm not sure I'd like that."

Surely, she wouldn't. But I really think it would be best for me.

I walk over to her and pull her close to my chest and she pushes me back. I let the space back in between us and try not to lose it.

"Is this song okay?"

"What does it matter? I don't want to dance."

I point to her socked foot still tapping. "You love this song."

She points to my foot tapping. "You love it, too."

"Of course."

"It's a lovely song."

She's dancing and so I am. Three socks move in space. The room gets smaller. I reach through it.

"Can I hold you?"

Maya keeps dancing and it's best I let her.

Diary Entry #332

A boy with rainbow braces and a
rubber-band bracelet wants to take a
photo with me. His parents lean against
a storefront whispering in the background,
no idea who I am and dubious as to
what I've done to deserve their son's
smile. I go through the routine with
the boy. I bend my knees a little more
than is comfortable so that our eyes
are more aligned, so the exchange feels
less like one between a man and a child
and more like one between two humans.
For this part of the exchange, I'm proud
of myself. For what follows, not as much.
I ask him his name as if it matters,
say it loud as if ~~spoken~~ once spoken I'll
never forget it; Tyler, Oliver, Pat. It can be
anything. And each time I lie to myself
I tell myself that this is the one
I'll never forget—

that this is the moment and the
face that I'll remember forever. Now
his phone comes out and he extends
his arm, and we take a picture with
our cheeks close together. And sadly,
this is the real moment, the one that
I'll actually remember forever: when
we stare ahead ahead, not at each other,
and I get to see the parents instead
of the child, I get to see them
outside of this moment odd moment,
I get to see someone just as confused
as I am, pondering the same question
I will ponder nine more times
today and nine more times tomorrow —

"Who is this this almost-thirty-
year-old-man? What has he done
to deserve this treatment, this kind
of love?"

T. S

An Accomplished Man

Across from him: three older women studying for a nursing exam, a young man reading a textbook on environmental policy, a social worker practicing sign language.

In front of him: Instagram likes, a silly book, a paycheck from Youtube.

Inside of him: eleven kinds of guilt guilt guilt guilt guilt guilt guilt guilt guilt guilt guilt.

Dear Pen Pal

Dear Pen Pal,

There's a burglar in my house.

I am hiding in my closet behind a jean jacket.

I am scared.

I am nervous.

I am starting to think that I grabbed the wrong item off my nightstand.

Who Said It?

1. "I'm bored."

    a) Bugs Bunny during duck season.

    b) Your Dad listening to Neutral Milk Hotel.

    c) Kid at the arcade who blew all his quarters on *Dance Dance Revolution* during the first five minutes of a three-hour birthday party.

    d) Porn star playing spin the bottle.

2. "Pshh. What do I care if I'm hungover tomorrow?"

    a) High school science teacher the day her copy of *Planet Earth 2* came in the mail.

    b) Recent sweepstakes winner of a lifetime supply of Blue Gatorade and Advil.

    c) Todd.

    d) Everyone in attendance at the Mesoamerican Calendar Appreciation Party on 12/21/2012.

3. "I don't get it."

    a) Thirtieth century music historian examining footage of EDC.

    b) Overly vocal leftfielder during routine pop fly to right.

    c) A candid movie review of *Eternal Sunshine of the Spotless Mind.*

    d) Half the party after you just spent twenty minutes arduously explaining to them how to play King's Cup.

History History

history history
tends to repeat itself

Sixteen Weeks Russian

"Who can tell me the three branches of American Government?"

No one raised their hand. It probably had more to do with the stigma attached to participating on the first day of community college than a collective cluelessness.

"Ok then, who can *not* tell me the three branches of American Government?"

A lonely hand raised four rows ahead of me. I'm sure this was followed by immediate regret. The spotlight shined down on his ignorance. I felt bad — and in a Moment dominated by uncharacteristically brave empathy, I raised my hand, too. I knew the answer. But I felt like I'd take some of the attention off this poor student in hopes that the teacher would tell us the answer, move on, and, you know, teach.

Instead, he singled us both out, and his voice morphed from college professor to military sergeant.

"How do you not know the branches of your own government!? I can't wait to hear your excuse. I always like to start my lectures with a laugh."

My plan was to just use whatever excuse the other student used, knowing I was in too deep to confess that I actually knew the answer: executive, judicial, legislative.

He spoke up. I listened closely so I could mimic his response, making us equally embarrassed. His voice stuttered out of the gate, and then, in an unassimilated Russian accent, he says, "I am sorry professor, you see, I live in Russia my whole life. I move here because I really badly want to learn the American way of life and government and one day have American life."

He's in the clear.

I'm fucked.

The professor turned his attention toward me after giving his Russian protégé a smile of approval. I wanted to say, *just kidding*. I wanted to tell the professor that I was just being a nice guy. But I was past the point of no return. I opened my mouth and prayed something good would come out. And in a Moment of rare, verbal brilliance I uttered, in a somehow perfect Russian accent, "Yes, we are brothers, brothers from Russia. We really want to learn these American branches of government of USA."

The professor started a slow clap and soon the entire lecture hall welcomed us to our new country. My Russian brother looked at me. Never before have I seen someone so confused. I winked at him, and he still had no idea what was going on. But he'd soon learn. Because for the next sixteen weeks — Tuesdays and Thursdays from 11:00 a.m. to 12:15 p.m. — I was Russian, studying abroad in my hometown.

@writerboy67

"Your writing style reminds me of — "

"Ah, yes. Updike. Chekhov. Salinger. Carver. Joyce? Yates? Lorrie Moore? Alice Munro? Tobias Wolff? Amy Hempel? Sherwood Anderson? Lydia Davis, surely!"

"Oh, no. I was going to say @writerboy67. His IG captions are fire."

"Of course."

Rapunzel: The Prequel

An Author and An Ex

I see my ex-wife's car parked on King Street. Stickers line the bumper: something about religion, something about politics, something about Bruce Springsteen being better than John Mellencamp. Nothing I agree with. When she insisted that she drive, I insisted she wait a minute: "Let me grab a jacket. One with a hood."

The license plate is the same. 6GD19C9. (I had this brilliant way of remembering it involving acronyms and philosophers' birthdays. She had this boring way of remembering it involving math.) The parking meter is flashing zeros, and I give it two quarters. Always warned her about credit cards. *What if you want a gumball?*

The back window is covered in dirt. I can write an essay with my fingertip. (And she said my MFA had no practical value!) What band was it that wrote an EP on a pizza box? And who's to say that this isn't my pizza box Moment? People passing by would stop and read it. A Literary Banksy, they'd think. Shakespearian Street Art, others might say. At the very least, it'll feel good to write. She might not like it, but she's never been the biggest fan of my work to begin with. What was it she said about my vows — too Chekhovian?

I ready my finger. There's so much to be said. My brain is doing that thing that got me into this mess to begin with, telling me to drop all responsibilities and write. I give in how I always do. I'm already five minutes late. What's a few more? I'll say something about a fender bender. I'll work it into the interview — rub the back of my neck and time a sigh of relief with their *please, take a seat*. Or better yet, I'll skip the job interview entirely, take a nap in Barnsdall Park. There'd be something commendable about that. Bukowski could explain it better. He saw the art in a man sleeping on a bench. My wife could never wrap her head around it.

The window is warm. My thoughts are fast. But my hand moves slowly.

And I am reminded, yet again, that infinity — the notion that there is so much to say — is just a romantic idea when it comes to writing. A novel in the head is hardly a Haiku in its execution. It's not just writers who know this. When a finger touches down on a dirty window, while there seems plenty of room to roam, there are only two ways to go: WASH ME or a penis.

And she's always said I was a better artist than author.

I decide on realism, making one hang lower than the other.

Diary Entry #21

The first thing people see when they google my name is an article I wrote about the anatomy of the forearm for a fitness magazine. I'd rather it be a photo of me naked or a rumor that I litter or a video of me drawing on a turtle with chalk. Those types of things don't hurt your reputation quite as much as this does in the literary world. An open affinity for health & wellness isn't a good look on an artist. I think if you can bench 225 you're no longer eligible to win a Pulitzer.

the publication that will haunt you forever.

Maybe i'll stage an interview where i say my favorite movie is **My Dinner** with Andre and that my ideal first date is a night at the theatre. Would they respect me then? Then would they call me an° artist? What if i°recited the speech from Joyce's The Dead at a dinner party? What if i Kept a criticism on 20th century German literature in my Jacket Pocket?

what if?

D.N

and your favorite musician is post-Bright Eyes Conor Oberst?

Kafka Getting into Character

"Can I help you find anything, sir?"

"Yes, I was wondering if you had a size medium in this giant insect costume?"

Is It Art*?

If you answer "yes" to 7 out of 10 of these questions, it MIGHT be art!*

Is it in a museum?

Is its target demographic fifty-six-year-old white guys with their shirts tucked in?

Is it at first underwhelming and dull, but then earns your appreciation after you take a semester long course on how to appreciate it?

Is the creator's name hard to pronounce?

Is it in black and white despite being conceived in an era of digital color?

Upon gazing at it, does it make you squint your eyes and gently stroke your beard?

Was it created by an alcoholic?

Does your French cousin think it's art?

When discussing it, do people use words like *dichotomy* or *juxtaposition*?

Is there nudity that doesn't turn you on?

---

*We do not claim to know what art is. People have made it very clear that we do not know what art is.

In the Garden my Grandmother Visits

In the garden my Grandmother visits there's a young man holding a
gun to his head asking for money *or else.* He's raised four dollars and
a few eyebrows. The gun is fake. It's my job to tell Grandma those
types of things: that the gun is fake, that the cab driver doesn't need to
see her ID, that the garden she's been visiting her whole life is on 4th
and K, that *my name is Charlie, your Grandson, don't you remember?*

Grandma smiles; she says she loves experimental art, loved it as
long as she can remember, goes on about how clever this young man
is for flipping the script on a robbery. Grandpa would call a person
like this a jackass. I'm still undecided.

Art suspends her Alzheimer's for a minute. I try not to get too
excited. She reaches into her coin purse for payment. She gives it to
me to give to him. Being a boy I'm familiar with being between a trans-
action. Mom to me to cafeteria lady. Dad to me to pinball machine.
Grandma to me to guy with gun to head. It's less than eighty cents
but heavier than a hundred dollars. I pour the coins into a small hole
he's dug by his feet.

He pulls the trigger and there's a loud pop.

He drops to the dirt and his tongue spills out of his mouth and
a light blue bullet (plastic) rolls toward a row of peppers (red). He
doesn't get up until Grandma finds a five. A true artist knows his
worth, she tells me.

Then she wanders off with a small shovel. I hand the man the five.
I tell him he'd make more money if he stood out on 17th Street.

He tells me it's not about the money. But Grandpa says it's always about the money, so again I ask the man what he plans to buy with all his money. He says that he doesn't *buy* things. He *invests* in his art. This doesn't answer my question. Again, I ask him what he plans to buy with all this money. I'm an artist, he says over and over. I'm an artist. I'm a goddamn artist.

"A real gun," I tell him.

"No, it's fake," he tells me.

"No. A real gun. You can buy a real gun with all your money," I tell him. "The show's a little bland."

He thinks it over and counts his money with his eyes like he's guessing marbles, and I worry I've told my best joke to a man who doesn't get it.

I go watch Grandma do her gardening, which consists of her digging small holes and saying, "What a nice hole I've dug." And at home I tell Grandpa not to give her anymore fives. He asks why. I tell him about the artist. I tell him about the gun and the loud pop. I tell him about my joke.

"Ah, now that's art," he tells me, needing humor now more than ever.

WE WILL NOT WASTE A PAGE TO DO THE SIMPSONS' CHALKBOARD GAG.

WE WILL NOT WASTE A PAGE TO DO THE SIMPSONS' CHALKBOARD GAG.

WE WILL NOT WASTE A PAGE TO DO THE SIMPSONS' CHALKBOARD GAG.

WE WILL NOT WASTE A PAGE TO DO THE SIMPSONS' CHALKBOARD GAG.

WE WILL NOT WASTE A PAGE TO DO THE SIMPSONS' CHALKBOARD GAG.

WE WILL NOT WASTE A PAGE TO DO THE SIMPSONS' CHALKBOARD GAG.

WE WILL NOT WASTE A PAGE TO DO THE SIMPSONS' CHALKBOARD GAG.

WE WILL NOT WASTE A PAGE TO DO THE SIMPSONS' CHALKBOARD GAG.

WE WILL NOT WASTE A PAGE TO DO THE SIMPSONS' CHALKBOARD GAG.

WE WILL NOT WASTE A PAGE TO DO THE SIMPSONS' CHALKBOARD GAG.

WE WILL NOT WASTE A PAGE TO DO THE SIMPSONS' CHALKBOARD GAG.

WE WILL NOT WASTE A PAGE TO DO THE SIMPSONS' CHALKBOARD GAG.

WE WILL NOT WASTE A PAGE TO DO THE SIMPSONS' CHALKBOARD GAG.

WE WILL NOT WASTE A PAGE TO DO THE SIMPSONS' CHALKBOARD GAG.

WE WILL NOT WASTE A PAGE TO DO THE SIMPSONS' CHALKBOARD GAG.

WE WILL NOT WASTE A PAGE TO DO THE SIMPSONS' CHALKBOARD GAG.

WE WILL NOT WASTE A PAGE TO DO THE SIMPSONS' CHALKBOARD GAG.

WE WILL NOT WASTE A PAGE TO DO THE SIMPSONS' CHALKBOARD GAG.

WE WILL NOT WASTE A PAGE TO DO THE SIMPSONS' CHALKBOARD GAG.

WE WILL NOT WASTE A PAGE TO DO THE SIMPSONS' CHALKBOARD GAG.

WE WILL NOT WASTE A PAGE TO DO THE SIMPSONS' CHALKBOARD GAG.

WE WILL NOT WASTE A PAGE TO DO THE SIMPSONS' CHALKBOARD GAG.

An Encounter

The girl in the puffy, red vest chews her gum like she's trying to break it. I'm scared if she misses the gum — if she miscalculates the trajectory of her teeth — they'll shatter against each other. I'm waiting for my coffee to cool and until then I'll keep watching this woman. Huh. Now, she spits the gum into her napkin. I suppose her speedy chews shortened the life of the flavor. Oh, I see. She needs to eat her lunch. She takes a bite of her sandwich. Tuna, I think. Oh, this is gross — she chews it just how she did her gum. She really puts her whole body into the chewing. Her hair is bouncing up and down from the turbulence of her jaw. She sets the sandwich down after each bite, as if she needs both hands free to chew. She plays with her hair a bit. It's curly and blonde. Her eyes are large and her eyelashes are short. She picks the sandwich back up. She rotates it a half turn and takes a bite from the opposite end that she started from. It appears she'll be tackling this thing from all angles. Strange. She sets it back down. She has a small freckle on the corner of her mouth. It's kind of cute. Wait. No, it's just a crumb. She wipes it off with the back of her hand. She stands up. Pink shorts, pale legs. She takes a step away from the table and then backtracks to grab her sandwich like it was her cellphone. Huh. She's walking over here — maybe to throw the sandwich away. Still chewing theatrically. Her feet aren't fully in her shoes. Her walk is a bit of a waddle. She's getting pretty close to me now. Her cheeks are stuffed with food like a child's cheeks filled with pool water ready to shoot. She swallows it down her long neck. She's right in front of me, looking like some sort of creature I can't take my eyes off of. She opens her mouth. Oh. Wait. Hold on... Okay, she just told me to stop staring at her. She's walking back to her table now. Oh. Crap. Okay, she just glanced back behind her. Fuck. She saw me still staring. She's coming back. Oh no. She looks angry. Oh gosh, she's yelling. She's asking me... yep... she knows, she knows I'm writing all this down. Hold on. Okay ya so she's trying to slam my computer dowN1. HSshe is sl';;apppinG my arnss. I shoueled go;.. Im try to save rhthis documen hopefully-I hith save. Sheees sho srong HE;LP!

Poetry

"I write literary fiction."

Critic: Nice!   Consumer: Eww.

"I write genre fiction."

Critic: Eww.   Consumer: Nice!

"I write psychoanalytic literary criticism."

Critic: Yay!   Consumer: What?

"I write Listicles."

Critic: What?   Consumer: Yay!

"I write poetry."

Pussy!!!

Nowhere to Sleep in Scotland

one dry bench, already taken

pee under the bridge, rain everywhere else

directions to my hostel, somewhere missing

Farewell, Honeymoon Phase

he showered

then

she showered

not in any specific order

just one

and then

the other

Everything was Packed

The light didn't fill up much of the room. It was enough to show the smoke stains on the ceiling, the black Sharpie mark on the purple wall, and the penny glued to the floor — all of the things that bothered her the past three years.

"Don't be so bothered. I'll clean it up," he always said.

"You always say that," she always said.

She took a sip from a gallon of apple juice but didn't swallow. She walked to the window and opened the blinds and slipped two painkillers between her lips. She let them float in the warm apple juice like astronauts while she looked down at a rented, red minivan in the driveway.

She filled the gas tank last night. If she just left, she wouldn't have to stop until Mill Valley. Her rusted bike was fixed to the back. Her picture frames were wrapped in warm blankets on the passenger seat. Her books were shelved on the back seat — her favorites even buckled in. Their mattress was tied down to the top. She could have it; he'd get a new one. They agreed on this the last time she tied it down to the top of a rented car.

She swished the pills in the juice from cheek to cheek.

She thought, *I've packed everything but painkillers and a gallon of apple juice*.

She thought, *I really got it right this time*.

She swallowed. And soon after,

she floated off.

Diary Entry #559

She didn't say she was leaving me,
she said she was demonstrating
her freewill. A philosophical break-
up this time. What an artful scheme.
She got to break my heart AND
feel righteous in doing it, as
if I was just the tedious
stage-one-boss in her game
of ~~personal~~ personal growth.

Now I'm eating pretzels and
crying and watching my dog
nap on the rug near the
front door. At least my dog
has never left me; although,
who's to say she wouldn't
if her paws could navigate
doorknobs & gate latches.

Which has me thinking, maybe
freewill isn't so philosophical;
maybe it's anatomical— a
byproduct of a capable body,
an offshoot of opposable thumbs.
Ah-ha! My girlfriend didn't
delicately dissolve a relationship
on metaphysical grounds, she
dumped me with dirty human
hands!

But I understand.

We all need to put things
into whatever words make
us feel best.

D.N

She Just Kept Running

I whisper in Jane's ear across the center divider, "Don't forget the olives."

"Fuck off," Jane says under her breath. "And a side of olives," she says timidly toward the drive-thru menu.

Then comes the routine. It starts with the Carl's Jr. employee repeating *Olives?* several times and Jane repeating *Yes, Olives* several times. The word Olive exceeds its annual word count within fifteen seconds.

That's Jane's most hated *Lifetime Bets*. A *Lifetime Bet* is a thing we created when we were sophomores in high school. It's a simple bet. But the consequences last a lifetime. They aren't horrible consequences, rather subtle annoyances that you spend a lifetime trying to learn to live with — like the *olive* bet. Ever since Jane missed a three-foot putt in mini-golf, she's had to ask for a side of olives whenever ordering food.

We pull up to the window and Jane hands over almost the exact change, shorting the minimum wage hero a penny. *Power Move*, she calls it. Jane grabs the brown bag, pokes in all the bubbles on her soda lid, and takes a bite that separates herself from all skinny girl stereotypes before throwing the car into drive with her elbow. She's halfway through the burger by the third streetlight. Despite Jane looking like she has just bartered for a Grateful Dead record at a Gluten Free Garage sale, she eats like The Steelers offensive line.

Jane looks at me with her mouth open wider than her eyes and then back at the road, "What's your favorite color? Who's your favorite band? Do you want a piece of gum?" This is Jane reminding me that she's not the only one who has to live with the splinter pains of a lost *Lifetime Bet*.

I answer her question with undisturbed loyalty to our system: "Brown. Hoobastank. I don't chew gum."

Brown became my favorite color when Jane beat me in a best-out-of-a-hundred game of *Rock, Paper, Scissors*. Hoobastank became my favorite band when Jane legally changed her middle name to Archytas (her favorite Greek thinker). And I became the weirdo that declines a stick of gum — the bets were tailored to make me a horrible first date — when I bet Jane she couldn't finish three beers before the end of Don McLean's *American Pie*.

She finishes the last bite of her burger and asks, "Why do I hang out with you?"

"Because I'm the only one who hates school dances as much as you."

That night, instead of going to our Senior Year Homecoming, Jane and I sat in front of a muted TV eating junk food in dress pants. We had gotten all dolled up and took pictures to please my parents. The pictures actually came out pretty well despite Jane wearing a pair of her brother's slacks, combo'd with a bright yellow polo shirt. We plopped on the couch with no care of our clothes getting wrinkled. Our channel surfing landed on a women's tennis match. Without any planning, we started mocking tennis grunts. As my player served, I let out a "Aaaah!" Jane's player responded with a backhand, "Heeee-yaaahhh!" It was our version of Nintendo. Then, once the distinction between athletic grunt and animal sex noise became a blur, we started kissing — you know, the smooth and natural transition from grunting at a muted television. Kids kissing. It didn't mean much. One of us wished it did. But it didn't, she often assured me.

Then we stopped.

Jane looked at me. She was quiet. This happened when her thoughts got loud. You could always measure her brain activity by how wide her eyes were. When they were wide, there may as well have been a cartoon light bulb floating above her head. She'd often be doing something mundane, like eating pudding or putting her hair up in a bun, and then she'd have a philosophical rush that she'd have to publicly pontificate. In this case, her spark to speech was my boring kissing. She elongated her spine and squared her shoulders. She was tense, eagerly waiting for each word to make its way from her mind to her tongue. She didn't look like Jane. She was Archytas. Archytas in a yellow polo and baggy slacks.

She went on to tell me how the most beautiful times come when thought is absent because action appears mandatory. She told me, when we let our minds rest, we let our bodies live. She spoke the words of a hippie with the conviction of a preacher. To put her philosophy to practice, she came up with the idea that we create an unplanned action for each other, an action that would let our bodies live. On separate pieces of paper, we wrote a random "call to action" for the other person without telling them what it was. We folded them, exchanged them, and put them deep in whatever pockets we could find in our uncomfortably fancy pants, hoping to forget about it, and agreeing that the day we pulled it out we'd read it and complete it on the spot — with no contemplation. At that Moment we would be forced to act, and our bodies would come to life. Plus, she noted, we are both wearing shit neither of us ever wear, so it will be enough time to forget about the whole thing. Then we unmuted the TV to hear the actual grunts. It was always disappointing.

That was ages ago. After high school Jane traveled. She said she wanted to do it solo, to find her potential. She also wanted to find out if Archytas was right. The question always bothered her;

and science's answer didn't fulfill her. "*If I am at the extremity of the heaven of the fixed stars, can I stretch outwards my hand?*"

I heard she went everywhere, but noticed she never got around to coming back. She was always looking for the edge of her world, never too concerned that she was the center of mine.

Today, I get a call on Skype. It's Jane. A much older Jane. A hardly recognizable Jane. She's standing in a grocery store pushing around a red cart with a toaster and a wedding card in it. She angles the camera down at her high heels and the cuffed bottoms of the slacks she wore the night we didn't go to Homecoming. And now she zooms in on her hand holding my crumpled-up note in her palm. It's weathered, but the words are the same.

Take Off Your Shoes and Just Run

The camera bounces up and down during her race around the store and then she heads for the exit and then through the parking lot and then across the street and she just keeps running and laughing and smiling and living. Thinking nothing, feeling everything. Forty minutes later, there's a knock on my door and she's dripping in sweat, standing on soon to be blistered feet, with high heels in her hand, covered in a smile that looks like life.

A Talk with My Little Girl

"Dad, why are there height requirements for rollercoasters?"

"Otherwise there'd be no good reason to grow up, sweetie."

An Unfortunate Oxymoron

My daughter doesn't know what I mean when I say, "Family party."
She knows the two words, but together they don't make much sense.
She's more familiar with *family disaster* and *family emergency* and
family troubles, words often headlining her absence notes.

Close your eyes and imagine, I tell her: "Imagine a fire pit with
people around it. No one with anything to burn, just things to say.
Imagine a basketball hoop that's seen more skyhooks than jump shots,
more granny shots than layups. Red peppers filled with provolone
cheese and bacon, a pool filled with kids and inflatable flamingos.
Balloons popping, Dads pretending to take bullets to the chest, kids
laughing. Grandpa telling that one story again, no one listening to the
words, but everyone listening to his soft voice. Men saying I love you
to other men. Women doing the same. Grown-ups hugging. That's
real. They really did. They kissed one cheek, then the other. Then the
kids, we'd yell au revoir, not knowing what it meant, but knowing that
it made Grandma happy. Grandma would let the tears roll down her
cheeks so she could use both hands to wave. You only wipe away the
bad tears, she used to say. 'The good ones don't hurt, just tickle.' Can
you imagine that? A family enjoying each other. We really did. That's
just how it was. Promise."

My daughter opens her eyes. "A *family party*," she says incredulously.
"Yes," I plead.

She uncaps a red marker tucked behind her ear. It's a good one.
The type of marker the teacher makes you check out and return. The

marker your teacher buys with her own money and lets you know she bought with her own money — not the marker you'd find in our junk drawer at home. "*Family party*," my daughter says again. "We learned about that today in English."

"About what?" I ask.

"I forgot what it's called," she says. She brings the perfect red marker to her recess stained left shoe, and she writes the two words on her white soles: family-party.

"It's like jumbo-shrimp," she says.

His Heavy Arm Over Her Small Body

They stumble out of the bar and through the city, taking wrong turns, slipping on their
own steps, and following the social script of intoxication:
"You're drunk"
followed by
"No, you're drunk."
And the hollow romance goes on until they finally make it to his front door
and he grabs his key from his sock.

His room isn't fully dark, but dimly lit by an old lamp in the corner next to his bed. And
he hopes it's dark enough to keep her from seeing his sad life.
There's an unfinished game of Solitaire spread across the carpet.
There's a book of mazes on his desk.
There's a Hacky Sack on top of a Rubik's Cube on top of a cup of noodles.

They walk toward his bed, and he prays she doesn't trip over a shoe
or fall through a pile of clothes like a trapdoor.
A bag of Ruffles pops under her black heel.
She screams at the noise and falls forward into the bed and laughs.
She rolls over onto her back and shakes out her legs until she's barefoot.
He dives on top of her and turns off the lamp.

Words are few.
Some playful *hi*'s and *hey*'s.

Some compliments whispered.

And when they are done, they look at each other and embrace
the silence entirely.
The moonlight slices through the blinds and decorates her face.
Everything slows down.
But his thoughts speed up.

He thinks,
"There's a stranger in my bed and I just might love her."
And then he questions,
"How lonely must a man be to fall in love with a stranger in his bed?"

I'm fine, he thinks. *I'm not lonely*, he decides.

And the desperate-drunk-lonely-messy-man tries to believe
that if this stranger in his bed were to get up, grab her heels,
and call a cab,
he'd be fine with it.
He tries to believe it for as long as he can.
But soon,
he drapes his heavy arm over her small body and closes his eyes.
And each time she moves gently under the weight of his arm,
he grabs the sheet a little tighter.
And when she gets up to leave in the middle of the night,
he tells himself she's just using the restroom; and he falls back asleep
and waits for the flush to wake him.

It's Different When It's The Moon

It woke me up at 4 a.m., so I reached for my pen and paper beneath my bed to write a poem about it. But when I realized it wasn't the moon in the sky that woke me, that it was just the lamppost on the sidewalk, I redirected my reach toward a gym sock and laid it over my eyes like a sleeping mask. And instead of writing poetry under the moonlight, I did math under a streetlight:

6 a.m. minus 4 a.m. equals work in 2 hours, ugh.

Alive But Trapped

John Sebastian's *Daydream* played on the radio on the floor. My great-grandpa, Grompy, sat on the couch looking into the kitchen, watching me "bake."

I folded a piece of wheat
bread
and cut a semicircle in the center with a pair of
turquoise scissors.
When I unfolded the bread it had a perfect hole in the center,
just like a donut.
I glazed it with a thin layer of honey and sprinkled it with sesame
seeds, adding an element of creativity to my
dishonesty.

Then I bent down and picked up the fallen piece of bread from the cut
and stuffed it in my mouth — discarding the truth deep down in my stom-
ach.

"Got you a donut, Gromp."
"Oh, a donut. Nothing like a donut. Oh, handsome, handsome boy.
Thank you, thank you."

Grompy took a bite of the *donut* as he watched his small fishes
swim circles
in the fishbowl

in the sun
next to the kitchen window.

He slowed his chewing until his *donut* was just sitting atop his tongue.
"They might be hungry," he said.
"I'm sure they're hungry," he kept saying of the fish.
He looked at his *donut* and then again at his three fishes
swimming circles —
alive but trapped.

Grompy tried to stand up, but
he couldn't.
He looked at his legs thinking that maybe they had turned to dust.
But they were still there, and they looked fine and capable.

"You want up?" I asked, unfortunately aware of the motherlike tone
in my voice.
He tried some more to stand.
I pulled him up.

He walked to the fishes holding out his *donut* in front him,
smiling as if bringing a bone to a dog.
And when he finally got across the kitchen,
he dropped the bread into the fishbowl.
It belly flopped and stuck to the surface like a lily pad.
Each fish swam to the top of the bowl
to first nibble on it
and then ignore it.

But Grompy just saw the nibbles.
He saw the fishes swim up with their mouths open,
and then he turned his back with a smile and
slowly slid his feet across the tile toward the couch,
singing along to the radio through his travels:

what a day for a daydream
what a day for a daydreaming boy.

And while he moved toward his resting place,
the bread sank down toward the three fish
like a foot coming down
on an ant.

Drinking for the First Time

I knew,
after a drink
and then another,
that this night wouldn't be anything special.
It wouldn't be as memorable as my third-grade play or getting hit
in the tooth with a surfboard.
I'll look back at tonight and think:
"Was it before prom or after homecoming? Were we in Jason's
backyard or Franky's cousin's garage? Was my hand numb from
the cold can or the cold bottle?"
I know I'll never be able to distinguish this night from the other nights.

Because I'll make sure the other nights are so similar, starting just
the same as this one:
with a drink
and then another.

Diary Entry #401

I haven't had a sip of alcohol in twenty-one days. They have been the most boring days of my life, but the most competitive. I drank so much that it became dull, and I picked up a new hobby of being sober. I made it twenty one days sober because I didn't want to lose to myself taking a sip of alcohol. However, sobriety is a strange battle. You have to keep winning, day after day. My calender looks like this: war, war, war, war. And now I've almost forgotten the taste of defeat. The sweet sweet taste of defeat.

T.S

Coolest use of the word "Competitive"

Dude this was awesome.
I wanna hear more about
these competitive days.

Public Service Announcement

Running shoes with pants is cool again.

Shakespeare Sliding into Your DMs

My love, you are perfect in all ways and on all days.
You need no makeup in the morning and no dog filter in the evening.
Be certain, I will write you every night — until my thumbs get sore
and my battery dies.
And I'll tap twice on your pics for as long as they aren't with other guys.
I will sing you a song in perfect key.
Or if it's a love letter you want,
I can give you
the D.

Literary Party Games

▶ Take a drag from your cigarette anytime a Hemingway character mistreats a woman.

▶ Two sips of beer for each word you have to look up in *Infinite Jest.*

▶ Take a shot for every five drinks poured in *What We Talk About When We Talk About Love.*

▶ Do whatever drugs Kerouac tells you to do.

▶ Take off an article of clothing anytime Salinger says "trifle" in *Franny and Zooey* (this works for up to eighteen articles of clothing).

▶ Spin the bottle anytime Percy Shelly references the ruler of Egypt from 1279 BCE to 1213 BCE.

▶ Backflip into the pool every time you start dozing off during *To The Lighthouse.*

▶ Eat a Bagel Bite every time David Sedaris is way funnier than you.

▶ Prank call your ex when you realize you have no idea what Donald Barthelme is talking about.

▶ When you find yourself liking the company of fictional characters more than your friends and identifying with the narrator more than yourself, put the book down and go have some fun.

A Bad Movie

They asked us if they could turn our short story into a film.

"A movie?" we asked.

"Yes, a film," they said. "We'll make it a hit! We have this vision for your characters. We have this vision for new conflicts. We have this vision for your story. What do you say?"

"Do we have to watch it?"

Pythagoras: The One-Hit Wonder

Fan: "I love your theorem, Mr. Pythagoras!"

Pythagoras: "Thank you. And may I ask which theorem you are referring to? Many have been attributed to my name."

Fan: "You know! Your theorem! The famous one! The triangle one! The one everyone is talking about!"

Pythagoras: "Oh yes, that one. Did you hear I released new ones?"

Fan: "No."

Pythagoras: "Really?"

Fan: "Oh, Mr. Pythagoras. Can you please just say it for me? Can you please say The Pythagorean Theorem for me!?"

Pythagoras: "Very well. In any right triangle, the square of the hypotenuse is equal to the sum of the squares of the other two sides."

Fan: "OMG I love you!"

Pythagoras: "Would you like to hear another one? Maybe my latest Theorem of Proportions, or how about Pythagorean Tuning, or my concept of a Spherical Earth?"

Fan: "Can you do the triangle one again? I forgot to hit record."

Pythagoras: (sighs)

"Wait… why are we burying it?"

Before the Bus Started to Move

"Isn't any exit a fire exit if there's a fire?"

I keep that joke to myself and laugh under my breath as the bus driver preaches his *What To Do In An Emergency* speech with a passion that has me convinced he is the proud founder of the cookie-cutter spiel. It's interesting how an hour-long monologue about safety can be followed by the silent sound of sixty children not having a seatbelt to buckle. But hey, at least we won't swallow our gum when we get thrown out of our seat during a *Damnit, I Should Have Gone* yellow light.

The bus driver continues to prep us for our four-minute drive with an animated tutorial on how to use and how to not use the radio. Which I'd say is the equivalent to teaching a kid that $2 + 2 = 4$ and then teaching that $2 + 2$ doesn't equal 73.

"Can our seat be used as a flotation device?" I mumble to myself — but loud enough for Haley to hear. Either she doesn't get the joke or doesn't think it's funny or doesn't want to be seen acknowledging someone of my social status. But she raises her hand. And before being called on, she yells to the front of the bus, "In the case of an emergency, can our seat cushions be used as a flotation device?"

The aisle floods with giggles that overrule Mrs. DeMarco's firm requests for silence. She soaks in the laughter, lets it pull the sides of her lips into a smile. And she whispers into my ear, "You got the jokes, but I got the balls."

Skinny Dipping

Cheap earrings go in pockets, expensive watches in socks. Shoes set neatly, shirts however they land. The girls look good. I can tell by the boys' eyes.

It was a raise of hands. Mine was for spin the bottle. But it's believed by the group that bottles can't spin on sand.

The girls compliment the one with actual boobs, who plays modest, says it's because she got held back a year. The boys make fun of the one covering up with two hands, who jokes back, says he doesn't want it to drag in the sand. Everyone laughs. I tighten my belt buckle a notch.

"Has nothing to do with the naked part," I make sure each person knows. It's that I can't swim, I tell them. But the girls make a good point. "You can still have half the fun," they explain. And they help me take my shirt off. The boys try my pants, but I get them myself.

I'm naked, alone on the beach, staring at my feet, staring at an empty beer bottle, thinking, if we just paved a small area of sand with our forearms, packed it down and made it dense with our hands, and smoothed it out a little, the bottle would spin just fine, wouldn't it? I carry out the experiment just to prove it to myself.

It spins — no different than if still on the hardwood floors of my Dad's warm house.

He's the one who suggested the sleepover. I fought it, told him how sneaking out and meeting with girls had become a thing in my friend group. He insisted. Even offered to talk to the parents if he had to. I told him I wasn't sure. He told me to use the side door. "There's a bucket by the shed. Yellow or orange, I think. Flip it over. Make sure it's sturdy, you know. And use it to getcha' over the wall. The fence squeaks. It doesn't but tell 'em it does. And tell 'em I'm a light sleeper. Makes it more fun."

The bottle slows down. It fights for one more rotation: past the life-guard tower, past a broken boogie board leash, past sport bras and sandy socks. And then the bottle stops, pointed at the water and the moon above it. Dad would chalk it up to fate. I'd chalk it up to the ocean being pretty fricken' big. But it's his night. And so I do him a favor and believe in something bigger than chance.

I walk for the white wash. First like a penguin, my arms never leaving far from my body. And then suddenly like a kid — like a kid past curfew in the summer, like a kid who hasn't read books about stingrays and rip currents, like a kid who's never seen the news, like a kid not yet afraid of the world… like one of those kids Dad's always telling me about.

When the remnants of a wave hit my ankles, I stop, squeeze my eyes tight, and think of how I might swim if it were true that I don't know how. But when I dive in, my body swims how it always has, effortless and smooth, yet it feels different, like I've been doing it wrong my whole life, like I hadn't even told a lie, like I've just now found my stroke.

Nature (2019)

A Young Boy and a Girl Who Doesn't Need Him

Murphy tried to figure out how to work the keg; Murphy drank a cup of foam.

"Wanna go down the hall?" he asked Vera. "I heard there's a waterbed," he added with a recently practiced wink.

Vera looked at him and at the foam in his cup and at the soft hair above his top lip and at his flat chest and narrow hips. He looked like a boy who loves rollercoasters, a boy who sits in the backseat of his Mom's car and tries to get 18-wheelers to honk their horns, a boy who brings a baseball glove into the ballpark, a boy who picks on girls like Vera until they develop breasts — a boy who waits until he's thirty-seven to become a man.

"I'll meet you back there," she whispered into his ear.

And as Murphy started to strut to the backroom of the party, Vera started to walk home. And when she thought about the new batteries in her vibrator in her sock drawer, she started to jog.

Also, Joan of Arc had Club Feet

The girl — the one wearing her Grandmother's jacket and the shoes that look like recess — walks to school hoping to be left alone. The boy — the one no different than the others — approaches her. His plan: show her the cool thing he can do with his pencil, tell her the joke about the kid with no eyelids, point to a house and say he toilet-papered it last week.

But she executes *her plan* first, yelling *facts* about geography and history: "Did you know that Brazil is in Rhode Island!? And that in 1441 potatoes became the state bird of Japan? Also, Joan of Arc had club feet!"

She found that this made boys leave her alone quicker than if she said, "Leave me alone."

Leave. Me. Alone.

Those strange words

in that strange order —

I love riddles!

is all the boy would think.

God's Spam Folder

9%: atheists praying to blend in

91%: football players on the winning team

Ostentatious Things I Say that Make Me Hate Myself

Ostentatious.

I'm fasting till 8:30.

The writing takes a dip after season 7.

I brought my own cup.

I saw a Ted Talk about that.

I liked their old stuff better.

Was that peer reviewed?

I don't believe in Kindles.

This? I can't remember, some random thrift shop, probably.

Ya, but it wouldn't be a two-party system if people weren't scared to vote third party.

In this case, you're probably better off with ibuprofen over acetaminophen.

Gas station sunglasses protect your eyes just as well.

I only use my phone for emergencies.

I believe in the *Historical* Jesus.

It's easy if you memorize the algorithm.

Penalize (pee-nol-ize).

I don't do dairy. People shouldn't do dairy.

I don't support their brand.

The science behind it is pretty neat.

Cambria just looks cleaner than Times New Roman.

I actually came for the opening band.

Another New Year

My wife wants to be sober this New Year's Eve, and I'm casting all my votes against it. Her plan is to stay dry and prepare a dinner that to me seems tiresome, with fresh ingredients and measuring cups and wine used for cooking not drinking. Each time she pours the merlot over the pan, I say, "You're doing it wrong." And I grab the bottle and take a long pull to remind her what wine is for — hoping her affinity for alcohol comes back to her as naturally as slipping into ice skates after a few warm winters in a row.

Soon enough, her sobriety slips, and the night gets a bit smoother.

She turns off the oven and the stove and takes a sip of the wine, and we open a bag of chips and do circles in the living room. After some laps she drops back into the couch with a sigh of relief, like she's sinking into a hot bath. "Feels good," she manages to mumble. Her slurred speech soothes me. I follow it into the couch and curl up against her and breathe in her strong breath.

I take a sip from the wine and pass it to my perfectly drunk wife, perfectly slouched so that we look exactly the same height, the top of her head no higher than mine. What a feeling. And in noticing this, I pass her a kiss as well. She takes a long pull and laughs. We hand the bottle back and forth — her lipstick decorating the rim with each sip, my chapped lips drying off the saliva she leaves behind. A team, I think. We look pathetic, she decides. We are enjoying ourselves, I remind her.

It isn't much we get to enjoy ourselves. Francine sculpts during the night — recreations of Terracotta Warriors and interpretations of the Venus de Milo, things like that — and during the day she gives physics lectures across the freeway at the University of Santa Barbara. The times she sells a sculpture, we go out for a nice dinner. She raises her hand for the check like she's excited to see how expensive it is. And she pays it with no problem. "It's no problem," she never forgets to say as she reaches for her purse. It gives her some sort of feeling. Makes her chest feel bigger and her shirt feel tighter.

(I work at a pool shop. Sell pool toys — giant inflatable flamingos, things like that.)

But now we are drunk and enjoying ourselves. We talk back and forth. She smiles at the things I say. I smile at the things she slurs. Nothing she says is smart or sophisticated. "Isn't cheese great?" "I don't understand people who have reptiles for pets." "What are ballerina shoes called again? Are they just called ballerina shoes?" It's perfect. And we close our eyes. It's not often we close our eyes and things are perfect.

But time fixes everything, even what's good.

I wake up from the quick doze, and she's in the kitchen with a coffee in one hand and a frying pan in the other. She's using the fresh ingredients, measuring cups, and a new bottle of wine for cooking not drinking. I pick up the bag of chips by my feet.

I stay on the couch. I stare at the TV watching a man with a microphone in New York City doing his best to convince viewers that a new year is something special. I can hear my wife behind me, prob- ably standing tall. Being productive. Cooking things. Washing things. Focused on a task. Accomplishing things. I can hear all these things behind the sound of chips crunching between my teeth.

From different rooms, Francine and I shout the final sixty seconds, each number lowering in count and ascending in volume, almost as if we were expecting something to explode and burn our home to the ground.

And between fifteen and fourteen she asks, "Just us this year?"

Well, actually, she says it like this: "Just us this year." Happy and thankful. A part of me knows she's happy and thankful. But I hear it, maybe through some insecurities, like a question. "*Just* us this year?" And now it's ringing in my ear like a complaint. "*Just us* this year?"

And now I wonder how long she has been holding that in — how disappointed she must be with *just us* this year.

So I count the last numbers even louder, so that even if someone were knocking on the door, a man better than me, a fan of her sculptures wanting to shake her hand, a man in a suit telling her she's won the Nobel Prize in physics, or a firefighter yelling for her to evacuate — she'd just hear me and the numbers coming out of my mouth, counting us into another new year.

And next year, I'll count through cupped hands. And the next year, I'll bark through a traffic cone. And the years after that: a microphone, a megaphone, a voice too tired, a house burned down, a wife five-foot-three, sells bath toys — rubber ducks, things like that.

The Howl Inside

Fun at first. A little boring now. Some fun again. Back to boring.
Mostly boring. Occasionally not boring. Boring some more.
Angry with being so bored. So bored being angry sounds fun.
Two people in love. The voices in their heads howling:
"FIGHT, FIGHT, FIGHT!"

The Full Length of the Wall

I watched him do it — down there in the alley beside our house. "Up to no good," my wife said. "Can you handle it, Sam?" she asked of me. "I'll handle it," I told her. But I just watched. I watched this tall man from our bedroom window standing in the alley, near our things, near my wife's car she's almost paid off, near the flowers finally blooming from finger-painted pots, near my daughter's purple tricycle we won in a raffle just last week, near all the things a husband is supposed to protect. I opened the window and leaned my head out. I cleared my throat to sell it to my wife that I might have it in me to yell, just how a man has it in him to yell. But I just watched. I watched this man spell his name with pee on our red brick wall. He had two hands on it. He moved left to right, knees slightly bent and angled outward so that his jeans wouldn't drop any further. His long flannel was pulled up and stuffed between his teeth. His hips thrusted forward like he was doing the limbo. He shuffled the length of the wall like a number of things that might shuffle the shoreline: a fisherman, a photographer, a life-guard — no, not just a crab. He traveled a great distance, something I've never had to do being given such a short, weak name: Sam. But this guy, he really moved. The full length of the wall, like I've said. Two hands on it, like I've said. And just like that, it was over. He opened his mouth and let his shirt hang. Pulled up his pants, buckled his belt. He stepped back from the wall. Centered himself in front of his work. Admired it briefly. Pulled out his phone to take a picture. Held the camera sideways, had to. The wall lit up, eleven letters dripping down red bricks: Constantine. Now that's a name.

A Look Through
My Second Grade Yearbook

Tanner Sampson
Tanner Sampson had a blue cast and was from St. Louis. On his first day, a kid asked, "How'd you break it?" and another asked, "Do they have school in St. Louis?" Everyone signed his cast at recess. He was an instant hit. Lucky guy.

Luke Mather
Luke Mather was sick and was in a wheelchair. Girls would fight over who got to push him up the ramp on our way to the assemblies. If I ever broke my leg, I wouldn't use crutches. I'd go straight to the wheelchair.

Everett Thomas
Everett Thomas knew what cocaine was. He also knew to laugh when the teacher told us to flip to page 69. His clothes were always dirty. He walked home from school by himself and even bragged that he wouldn't "go straight home." My Mom was at the curb thirty minutes before the bell rang.

Connor Robertson
Connor Robertson was short and had black spiky hair. He didn't even need hair gel. "It just stays up," he told everyone. He got all the love letters. They'd tell me, "Pass this to Connor."

Sophia Saben

Sophia Saben's Dad was a pitcher for the Red Sox. She was blonde and everyone liked her. A secret admirer gave her a hundred dollar bill on Valentine's Day. It was a big deal. I wish I'd thought of that.

Bobby Ennes

Bobby Ennes slid into bases and dove to catch balls. Some people thought he gave Sophia the hundred bucks. Smart kid.

Troy Fields

Troy Fields had a nickname. Gecko. His Mom brought him McDonald's for lunch one day. I traded him my sandwich for three fries.

Kurt North

Kurt North's Dad was a tattoo artist. Kurt had some of his Dad's talent. He would draw things in class and when someone would say, "That's so good," he'd say, "It's just a sketch." When I drew things in class I'd get in trouble.

Stanford McArther

Stanford McArther's Dad came into class for reading groups on the same day as my Dad. His name was John. He had a Scottish Accent. My Dad spoke well, not too exciting though.

John Ortolf

John Ortolf mooned Travis Smith at his birthday party. I didn't see it happen and wanted to yell, "Do it again," but didn't have it in me.

"Hey, what are these things even called?"

Fake Facts that Feel Real

▶ Automated doors evolved from chivalry's death.

▶ 65% of food waste in America is from Tina not eating the food.

▶ Every time you leave a dumpster open a raccoon is born.

▶ The average game of golf lasts approximately way longer than you want it to.

▶ Sleeping medicine is just the noise of a fan condensed into a pill.

▶ The most difficult part about being in a polygamous relationship is finding a big enough tree to fit all your initials.

▶ Birds and car washes are colluding.

▶ New batteries come from remotes.

▶ Gas station clerks have a minor in cartography.

▶ When a girl cleans her sheets it's responsible. When a guy cleans his sheets it's suspicious.

▶ The people who need megaphones the least have them the most.

▶ 90% of people who read *The New Yorker* are just trying to figure out how to get in *The New Yorker*.

The Pillow We Fought For

My Grandmother — who had seven middle names that I spent more time trying to memorize than my vocab words — sang a French nursery rhyme while she rubbed an aloe vera plant across my cousin's back. "Watch this," he said that morning. He took off his shirt and laid on his belly in the backyard on the red bricks by the pool, staying mostly still under the sun, waving his hand occasionally toward the tall emerald greens to shoo away their shadow. By afternoon his white skin was slightly pink — barely burned. Yet, he got the works: the aloe plant tickling his back, Grandma's French song and soft voice tickling his ear. Grandma's lap was the pillow we fought for. He tucked his hands between the couch and her legs. He grinned at me and winked. Then he turned his wink into sleep, and I walked home and played with a red ball on a string.

The next day was foggy. The sun took the day off; so, I took a pot of boiling water and poured it over my bare chest. I ran across the street to Grandmas, grabbed the aloe plant from the corner of the courtyard, and knocked on the door. My skin was falling off my chest. Grandma knocked the plant out of my hands, cursed in a foreign language that sounded too unpleasant to be French, and rushed me to the ER, where men talked to me in deep, unrhythmic voices and touched me with cold, latex hands. I got the works: the intravenous antibiotics, the 800mg ibuprofen, the IV fluids, and the synthetic skin.

I'd miss weeks of school. I'd miss two plays, a student vs. teacher softball game, a standardized test, eight vocab lists, and ninety-six vocab words — just enough to clear up space in my grade school lexicon to be able to memorize something more important, to finally be able to put all my energy toward my independent studies and be the first grandchild to call Grandma by her full name: Nicolle Reneé Andrea Adele Antoinette Gabrielle Clemence Corsiez Lipscomb.

Those Things that Need to be Talked About

They looked down at their drinks the way two people do when they can no longer talk about those things that need to be talked about.

The couple's lips played magnets with the moonshine. Then it went down: like a sunburned back thumping down a dry waterslide.

The couple slid their empty glasses to the center of the table as if they were both dealt a 2-7 off-suit.

The girl — in the comfort of her mind — played around with the words coming from the jukebox. She rearranged them and changed a few. She came up with:

slit your wrist with my broken dreams

That's poetic, she thought. Moody and melodramatic, but poetic. That should be in a poem, she decided.

The boy played around in his head, too.

He tried to remember the name of that actress he used to masturbate to in junior high.

It started with an *E*,

he thought.

Or was it a *V*?

Fourth Grade Stitchery Report: Project Joshville

The smartest kids stitched Wyoming and other states of similar geometric simplicity. The dumbest kids did Rhode Island, feeling as if they got away with something clever, not understanding what Mr. Caps meant by the states being stitched to scale. The most artistic kids did Hawaii and Florida and Michigan — the states with the most opportunity to showcase underfunded and underappreciated aptitude for the arts. The two boys who held hands did Massachusetts. The girl who fed a horse a carrot during spring break did Texas. The most popular kids all agreed to do New York, so when asked which state they chose, they could respond in a deep voice they'd meet again after puberty, "Where Brooklyn At?" And I, being the most innocent and imaginative kid, stitched Joshville.

With tubes coming out of his arms and needles going in, my brother told me that Joshville was his next stop. My parents confirmed this with me as we watched that black car take him there.

That black car. I remember thinking it drove too slow. Too slow to make it to Joshville. But my parents said it was okay. They said you can get anywhere at any speed.

"But Kentucky is two thousand miles from here. You can get two thousand miles going slow?"

"Yes," they told me.

"But what about four thousand miles? Can you get four thousand miles going slow?"

"Why not," they told me.

"This slow?" I asked, moving my body in slow motion down the steps of the church and through the crowd of crying family and friends, who — in line with funeral etiquette — had also downshifted the pace of their actions.

"Why not," my parents said again.

And then they dropped me off with neighbors I hardly knew while they attended the burial. "Fred and Alice," my parents had to remind me. "Fred and Alice," I repeated to myself.

They turned on the television and talked over the commercials. Alice told me about heaven. About how it's like teleporting. You are alive, and then you are in heaven. There's no between. It's that quick, she said. Your brother's already there.

Fred told me about decomposition and the carbon cycle. He asked me if I've seen how long it takes for a walnut to break down. Now imagine a walnut in a casket, he said. Your brother will become part of the Earth, but it'll take some time.

When the commercials ended, Fred and Alice held hands and used each other's bodies as pillows. Fred said that the woman on TV — the one holding case number 13 — was beautiful. Alice said that the woman holding case number 22 was much prettier.

"Who's right?" I wanted to ask.

When Howie Mandel told the women to open their case, they craned their necks to watch their own reveal, just as excited to see the number as the audience. I liked that about the show. No one knew the outcome. Everyone was figuring it out together.

"And where exactly is Joshville?" Mr. Caps asked, unamused by what he misdiagnosed as my *antics*. I held my project in front of my chest — frozen, much like the women holding cases on the television. The class stared, as if trying to thaw my body with their eyes. And when I didn't know what to say, Caps pressed harder, now leaning back into his chair, no longer grading me, more concerned with embarrassing me. "Okay, bud. How would we *get* to Joshville?"

"Slowly," I told him.

"Slowly?" he asked.

I craned my neck to watch my own presentation. I looked at Joshville. I studied it like a map. I thought about time and distance and death.

"Or quickly," I added. It doesn't really matter much, does it.

DiaryEntry#199

I've been spending a lot of time writing poetry lately. And I've been spending even more time trying to convince myself that I'm a better poet than I actually am. *(haha)*

If someone doesn't like my poems, it's probably b/c they haven't read Terry Eagleton's "How to Read a Poem," right? *(yes, Darren, yes.)*

D.∩

Poets, Publishers, And Birds

Dear Poet,
Thank you for submitting. However, we are unable to accept your poem at this time because it is not about a bird. Please try us again when you have written a poem about a bird or a small group of birds.

Dear Literary Journal,
Thank you for your feedback. I have one question in regard to the bird situation. When you say "small groups of birds" do you mean that I should write about a small quantity of normal sized birds or that I should write about individually small birds in an averaged sized group? Thank you.

Dear Poet,
Hello again. Concerning your inquisition about bird size and group size, either way works. Remember, there are no rules to great poetry! (Only than that we must invariably write about birds).

Dear Literary Journal,
I have taken your feedback and have written a wonderful poem about a bird of reasonable size. I have attached it below.

Dear Poet,

Please, no attachments. As stated in the submission guidelines, you are to write the poem in the BODY of the email.

(Note: We are temporarily closed to submissions, do not pay our contributors, and are second-guessing our bird policy.)

They Speak in Threes

It seems there are three things to say about the bluebird on the branch in the park.

An old man with an umbrella says:

Beautiful.

Lovely.

Wow.

A college student with a camera says:

Amazing.

Wonderful.

Unbelievable.

A girl with her parents says:

Awwwww.

Pretty.

Cool.

And the little boy with the wet hair and a missing sock says:

Ready.

Aim.

Fire.

His imaginary musket shoots him back three feet.

He secures it to his chest with an invisible strap and grins,

and he runs off to catch up to his father,

who still hasn't noticed him missing.

The Most Pretentious Man in the World

He climbs Mount Everest just so he can talk down to you.

He skips dinner because he already self-indulged.

He doesn't wear glasses; he wears two monocles.

You say, "Don't patronize me!" He says, "You're pronouncing it wrong. The etymology is actually quite interesting. You should look it up."

He calls his pajamas his sundown attire.

He gives beggars spare change to "stimulate the local economy."

Whatever side of the bed he wakes up on is the right side of the bed.

He thinks he deserves the first page in this book.

Guess what, guy. You get this page. You get this shit page sandwiched between two poems with unintentional octosyllables, tiresome enjambment, cheap alliteration, melodramatic refrains, and no discernable meter.

William Carlos Williams Isn't that Hungry

I have eaten

only one of your plums

that was in

the icebox

leaving you enough for a sufficient breakfast.

Forgive me,

for I wiped my purple plum hands on your new white dishrag.

I Get By

I get by with a little help from ~~my friends~~ pain meds.

Diary Entry #633

The self-confidence from the compliment I received eleven years ago is starting to wear off, so I'll stay in my room ~~today~~ and forego a walk along the grass and around the small lake outside the library; and who's to say that's such a bad thing ~~to say~~ stay in my room instead— come August the geese by the lake by the library get a bit aggressive. It's better inside. But my phone won't stop buzzing. People are loud in my house. Their noise ~~so~~ slips under the door and roars into my room. I've been trying to write for days now, but people won't stop being loud in my house. I can't think straight. My thoughts drop off the balance beam; they zig and zag like a seismograph. Am I spelling that right? The people won't stop ~~be~~ being loud in my house; maybe I need to think harder. My phone skips across my desk every so often as unsolicited calls and texts come in. I think, 'If the phone buzzes one more time I will pick it up and turn it off. Wait, no, I can't do that.

3 prob From me, Sorry.

A millennial can't turn his phone off. ~~People~~ People will worry, they'll think I've died." I don't know what the people in my house are conversing about, it all just sounds like noise; noise bouncing off one wall to the next, losing no speed. I can't imagine how awful it must be outside my room, sure it's loud in here, but at least I'm safe from the loud people and the angry geese.

T. S

Turn your phone off, man.
I'll make sure no one starts
planning your funeral.

The Happiest You've Been

Mom and Dad will hang the birthday banner when they think you've fallen asleep. It'll give them that same rush as old Christmases when all the kids were in the house, before bedrooms turned to offices and art rooms. One will put an ear to your door. The other will get down and peak under the crack (depends whose knees are feeling better). Turn your fan on high so they don't hear you reading, sounding out the word *unringleted*. Turn your lamp off early so they can get done in time to make fun of The Bachelor, the way he holds a rose like a crowbar.

You can hear them downstairs trying to figure out how to open the stepstool. Is it *pull the thingy, lift, and push* or *push the thingy, lift, and pull*? They give up and call the barstool into service. One climbs, the other holds. (Again, the knees.)

They hang the banner. First the three. Then the one. They knew well enough not to throw those numbers away after your third birthday. "We could use the one for his tenth and the three for his thirteenth," they must've thought. But never would they have guessed they'd put them in this order.

You're in your room. That same room. Walls that same green (Mom let you bring your tennis ball to Edward's Paints to hold up to the color samples). The carpet still has that one stain. The ceiling still has that one star. Shirt drawer still has the shirts. Sock drawer still has the drugs. The only difference in the room is that now there's no rule on your door being locked. Mom said the rule would be lifted when you graduated. Dad said it would be lifted when you could grow a beard. It evaporated naturally. You experimented pressing the lock with every finger and decided the thumb gave you the best rush, sent the best vibration through your hand, sent the sweetest sound of safety into the air, gave you the heaviest sigh of relief.

You stay up, using a carefully angled shutter and the moon as your reading light. You no longer stop to admire just how poetic that actually is. A book hovers inches from your face. Hands hold it loosely. Updike. *The Happiest I've Been.* Your thoughts try to grasp the title. You think of a memory. Mom and Dad would do a silly thing on holidays and birthdays and first days of school. They'd stand at the bottom of the stairs while you, your sister, and brothers waited at the top. They'd each have a microphone in their hand, unplugged from the karaoke machine (you used to sing *Short People* — the lyrics were mean but easy to memorize). Two hands on the microphone, Dad would dig deep into his throat and find his best Michael Buffer; Mom would lean closer to a Lawrence Tanter. They'd introduce your walk down the stairs. It would sound like this: "And at the top of the stairs, from Huntington Beach, California, as tall as the most unsellable Christmas tree on the lot, as heavy as a feather tied to a balloon, as old as that squishy tomato buried in our fridge, holding the handrail with the sweatiest hands in the family, make some noise for Benjamin Face-Red-As-A-Brick Johnson!" You'd walk down. Your parents would smile. Your siblings would cheer. You decide that is the happiest you've ever been.

Your eyes drift. Your hands slip. Page to the face and you're back again. 178. Third paragraph down. Find your spot and carry on.

Now it's not the moon but the sun. It warms up your forehead, taps on your eyelids and helps you out of bed. Still you don't see the poetry. You open your door and it snaps unlocked. It's enough to make you flinch.

The walk down the stairs is quiet. Breakfast is oatmeal. Use the brown sugar, convince yourself it's healthy. Take allergy medicine. Complain about how it doesn't work. Pour orange juice. Take a sip. Wonder why some people add ice. Proceed as normal. The banner is above you. You can feel it. Don't look up. Just eat. Chew. Swallow. You know how to do it.

Ah, but of course, a tickle in the nose. You look up. You can't help it. It's the anatomy of the sneeze. And now you see it. First the three. Then the one. The three looks like a pitchfork. The one looks like a spear. Together they stab you in the gut. You hunch over, sneezing into the collar of your shirt. No one blesses you.

Mom is helping a friend decorate her patio. Dad is paddling for a wave. Your brothers are in tall buildings in New York. Your sister can be anywhere. You're at the kitchen table of your parents' house, and it feels like there's nowhere else to go. But you know you have to try. That's all anyone's been saying. "You have to try." You look up at the numbers then down at your feet. Go on, find your shoes. It's been a while since you've worn any. They could be anywhere. Start looking.

The sidewalk is narrower than you remember it, feels like *Rainbow Road*. For most, this is a nostalgic Mario Kart reference, a comparison pulled from childhood, but you still play the game most mornings, so you find nothing unsettling about this choice of simile, about seeing a sidewalk as a multicolored raceway in space from which you can fall and lose everything. All of this is just to say a walk outside is a challenge, an adventure for you. Your balance has gotten worse. Your arms no longer swing how they should. Don't overthink it. Just keep walking.

Ahead of you is a lemonade stand. You guess maybe a hundred yards away. But you aren't the best with measuring distances. Think of it in terms of a football field, Dad would tell you. You played tennis, you'd remind him.

Instead you decide to measure with a clock. At this pace, you're sixty-three seconds away. You have just over a minute to think of an excuse as to why you will not be buying lemonade from these kids. The reasons are that you are not thirsty, have no money, and don't like talking to other people. But you've learned a good reason is different than a good excuse. Brute facts offer little comfort. "And it's comfort people are looking for in conversation," your therapist told you, "maybe this is why you write in the second-person when you're feeling distressed?"

You are thirty seconds away. Dad would call it a quarter of a football field, then he'd close his eyes and use both his hands to stuff tennis courts from the end zone to the twenty-five-yard line. "Two tennis courts?" he'd guess, not knowing much about tennis other than that Andy Roddick is married to Brooklyn Decker.

You are twenty seconds away. Close enough to see that the letters on their sign are forward facing. In cartoons the *e* would be backward. It's a cheap joke but it always lands. You think the kids missed an opportunity.

Ten seconds away from your first public interaction since you were twenty-nine. You can hear the leader of the children preparing her sales pitch. Still you have no excuse. Some might suggest you politely say *no thank you* to the children and keep walking, but you aren't ready for that. Instead, you pretend you do not hear her, and you kick a rock to maybe fool her into thinking you're a child like her, a child too young to be guilted in to buying lemonade, of the young age to find joy in such things as rock kicking and tire swinging (remember those days?). But she sees past it; maybe it's the beard, maybe it's the depression, maybe it's that you're humming a Dire Straits song from the '80s (just now realizing how many times Knopfler sung the word *faggot*).

She brings out the big guns: *excuse me, mister*.

She says something about the lemonade being for a good cause. And she waits for you to make the next move. It's fight or flight. This is what you do (my god, I can't believe this is what you do): you look into the distance and yell: "Sparky! Sparky! Where are you!?" And then you do this: you yell some more. "Oh, there you are! There you are Sparky!" And you chase down the street after your dog, Sparky, who is in fact not a lost dog at all but rather a hamster sleeping in a cage in the corner of your room. The pet was a purchase on necessity, on a to-do list between submit story to Wigleaf and cancel credit card. It was instructed more than it was desired. They say when it dies you will learn something. They say it'll be a lesson; it'll help answer life's big questions. But you suspect it'll help answer life's smaller questions: *hamster cage recyclable? hamster food resellable?*

You have an adrenaline rush from not buying lemonade. That gives you a quick laugh. A close call, but you've made it past obstacle one. Your recently prescribed walk around the block is proving to be doable. You've always had the feet for it. That was never in question.

You can see your destination: the plaza. It's still far in the distance, but you can already read the letters on the storefronts. You think about how great your eyesight is. You attribute this to all the television you watch — it's trained them so well! See, you've learned to reframe your bad habits in creative ways. This is part of the problem! Remember to bring that up on Thursday.

There are chatty townspeople along the way. But you've made it past prepubescent entrepreneurs, so you decide you have the strength to make it past anything. You really believe it. Please, remember that feeling of believing in yourself.

You get to H and 6th. It's the furthest you've been from home in some time. But then you see it. The worst thing you could see on a walk around the neighborhood. It's Mark. He's holding a baseball bat in one hand (in case of coyotes not sports) and a banana peel in the other. Your parents know Mark well, and Mark knows your parents well, so he's made it his mission to know you well. Mark will try to get into your head. This is what parents' friends do. They try to figure you out. Ask you stuff about things. Very intimate and personal things. Work. School. How tall are you now? Nothing is off limits. Mark will crush you. You tap out before he can. You sit on the curb, hoping you disappear behind the hydrant how a cartoon character does behind a tree, and you pull out your phone.

Your Uber driver asks why you need a ride such a short distance. You buckle your seatbelt anyway, and you say just this: "ankle."

And when you get out of the car you limp away, ashamed of your fake injury, but proud of where you've made it despite all that ails you.

"Rice!" the driver yells. "Rest, Ice, Something, Elevation."

You wish you could be fixed that easy. But listen. Try this. Pretend that you can. Scout out the perfect bench in the plaza to rest, to put your feet up, to begin the healing process. From there, watch the people live effortlessly. Like watching the poetry of a tennis match on the television, enjoy the play of life performed by the people around you. Make your hands into a square. Hold them out. Imagine they are the frame of a television if you have to:

FADE IN:

EXT. THE ARCATA PLAZA – MORNING

Kids hula hoop to a Grateful Dead cover band. Yoga mats turn to mattresses. Health Majors and Hacky Sack Minors drink straight from shared pitchers. Dogs not on leashes keep cars from speeding. Grass tickles toe tips hanging off the end of thrift shop bought Birkenstocks. Adults with office jobs braid each other's hair. Ezekiel bread is served to birds and stolen by squirrels. A degenerate pickpocket is given the benefit of the doubt, being dubbed a different title: man who has fallen on hard times. The sounds of squeaky swings float in the air from the schoolyard across the street. *North Coast Elementary*. But the letters on the marquee have been rearranged to say *No Toast Larry*.

Right here, on this bench, you watch your town enjoy the day; they are, as popular word choice would call them, blessed. Through mid-November fog, you watch people pretend that it's summer. How do they do it? It reminds you of that Creedence Clearwater Revival song. The one that goes, *Look at all the happy creatures dancin' on the lawn*. Some say Fogerty was on acid when he wrote it. You like to think he was on one of these benches.

Your nose tickles. You curse your Claritin-D. You look up. There's an airplane emerging from the old growth. And then a sneeze crashes down.

You think about the story you wrote about the little boy in the plaza woofing at airplanes. He sees anything that flies no different than birds. And sees birds no different than dogs. You are that boy, mistaking things that sing for things that bite. You become the boy even more and begin to bark at the sky. Let them stare. They've seen you do worse.

There's safety in this Moment. A feeling that the world can't hurt you — that it's them who need to beware. Quick, remember this feeling. Here comes a cloud.

An Assortment of Things

▶ My phone autocorrects a happy face to a sad face.

▶ I was having a bad hair day, so I avoided going places where I'd hear the National Anthem.

▶ What Todd orders at Italian restaurants has more to do with what he can confidently pronounce than what he wants to eat.

▶ I brought a grumpy customer a glass of water. He said, "I said no ice." I said, "I'm sorry… I'll go microwave that for you."

▶ My tent holds 3 to 4 people… depending if Kyle comes.

▶ My teacher said, "Don't come to my class on drugs." A student said, "Why not?" And I said, "It's a waste of drugs."

▶ How is it that a bottle of champagne can only get two people drunk but can get nine people hung over?

▶ I haven't met my new college roommate yet, but I know her name. I searched it on Facebook. 37 results came up. I messaged all of them: "Hey, I might be your new roommate… but probably not."

In the Bathroom

In the bathroom I fix my hair

In the bathroom I hide from relatives

In the bathroom I pee

In the bathroom I brush my teeth

In the bathroom I notice a light bulb needs to be changed

but I'll wait for someone else to do it

In the bathroom I check my hair

In the bathroom I shower

In the bathroom I poop

In the bathroom I question the order of my previous two tasks

In the bathroom I look at the dry spots on my elbows

In the bathroom I put more gel in my hair

In the bathroom I blow my nose

In the bathroom I mess with my hair some more

In the bathroom I brush my teeth

In the bathroom I think about flossing

In the bathroom I check my hair again

In the bathroom I just put on a fucking hat.

Lint

For lint I'm going to give up mispronunciation.

Thesaurus

When someone says *for lack of a better word*
I want to slap them in the face with a thesaurus.

Diary Entry #500

I copied Tobias Wolff's "An Episode in the Life of ~~Professor~~ Professor Brooke" by hand on a yellow legal pad to see what it would feel like to write something great. At the gym I loaded the barbell with four plates on each side to see what it would look like to be strong. And at home I closed my eyes, crossed my legs, and pressed my palms together in front of my chest, chanting, "ommm, ommm, ommm," to see what it would sound like to be a peaceful man, but all I heard was: "nice try! nice try! nice try!"

D.↷

this is interesting, might be a story here

What Is Who Is

I've heard of people going out to live in the deep woods. I've heard of people practicing Transcendental Meditation for six hours a day. I've heard of people chanting *GOD IS ALL, AND I AM NOTHING* under their breath until it sings involuntarily in their heart. I've heard of people doing all sorts of fanatical things to reach that state, that egoless state where their insignificance relative to the timeline of the universe is recognized and embraced, that state where earthly objects (their bodies included) are nothing of importance.

I go on this transcendental venture as well. Every night I watch *Jeopardy*. Channel 7. It does the spiritual labor for me. It teaches me my place in the universe. I turn it on and from my couch I learn that I know nothing, that I am full of nothing, that I have no knowledge of anything. "You know nothing. You are small and insignificant," says the game-show-sermon. Answers unknown to me roll by. And for these Moments I truly do feel like nothing. Lowly. Egoless. Humbling Floating.

Oh, but when I finally get one right.
What is this feeling.
Who is this genius in the reflection of the television.
Where's my crown, Trebek!?

An Idiot Wishes He Wasn't: 19 Across

I'm wearing this ugly hat that makes my face look too big for my head. It's a part of my strategy to look worse-looking than I am. The worse you look the higher your intellectual potential. You notice that? Freeman Dyson. So smart. So weird looking. The guy next to me. Handsome. Nice face, nice smile. Dumb as dirt. I'm sure of it. Also, you should see this jacket I'm wearing. It's ninety degrees out and I wear this jacket. Long. Green. Holes in all the right places. Hides my healthy physique. Makes me look a little sick, extra smart. I blow my nose a lot, too. Big ol' blows. Not cute. I feel like that's something Einstein would have done. I don't turn my back to those near me or walk to the restroom. Just blow. Stuff it in my pocket when I'm done. Just like Einstein probably. I get irritated at people rather quickly, too. People whispering too loud, I'll shush 'em. Don't care. I've heard of some smart men with short tempers. And my teeth. Strategic neglect has gotten them to a perfect shade of yellow. A lost retainer has given them some character. A smart person wouldn't bother with the superficiality of perfect teeth. So I'm here in the library looking smart, staring off into deep thought. Deep deep thought. So focused on thought. Looking like a genius, I'm sure. Thinking. Thinking. Been thinking for hours. *What's a three letter word for a flightless bird*?

I'll Give You a Dollar If You Tell Me I'm Smart (Word Play)

Foreign Language

I filled out a job application this weekend.
It asked, "Do you speak a foreign language?"
I said, "Depends who's asking?"

Voltaire Spoke French

I was in Paris at a local bar I couldn't pronounce the name of.
This woman took a sip of her wine and a drag from her cigarette
after pontificating to her boyfriend for quite some time.
I said, "Ah, that sounds like something Voltaire might say."
"Excusez moi?"
"Ya, ya, that too!"

Mysteries with Freddy

Freddy brushed away the dust from the treasure chest and read
the cryptic code engraved in ancient writing.
He said, "It's a surreptitious code."
I said, "What does *that* mean?"
He said, "It's a secret."
I said, "Come on, just tell me."

A Brief Interview with the Clever Novelist

Q: "Why is it that you often write about pain and suffering?"
A: "I don't want to talk about it."

Instead of a Tombstone

I'm wearing the yellow, oversized socks my sister gave me six Christmases ago. She laid them under the plastic tree beneath a beach towel — those Decembers, nothing was safe from being turned to wrapping paper. We gave gifts in Mom's grocery bags and Dad's cooking pot. We gave gifts in our pillow cases and favorite cereal box. And with the one three-dollar gift we gave each year, we gave a three-sentence speech: "You might grow sick of me," my sister said as I tossed aside the towel like tissue paper. "You might grow tired of this town, and you might even grow into a new person. But you'll never grow out of these oversized socks."

But this December the trees around me are real: fog on the needle tips, no gifts underneath. I can feel the forest behind me and see the ocean in front. I'm sitting in the sand. It feels like I'm sitting in a puddle. Christmas should be spent on carpet. I can feel the cold seeping through my gloves and through my jeans. But my feet still feel warm, like they've never left home. The tips of my socks look like duck bills, flapping far past my toes. Past my feet is the cold water of the north coast, not a warm fire from back home. The crashing waves remind me of the crackling wood. But the silence between them is much longer. There are Moments when I think the next one might not even come at all.

There's a hand on my head that I've been mistaking for my hood. A throat clears and now I turn around. Hovering above me is a young woman with old eyes and a goofy smile. She pulls away suddenly and says, "You're it!" She sprints away from me and down the beach, which at this hour of the night looks more like a desert. My new instincts — the ones I've grown into — tell me not to chase a woman in the night, or at any hour for that matter. But my old instincts — the ones I've grown out of — pull me to my feet and throw me across the sand. I chase her laughter like it's something I've lost. I run like a child. Not to get in shape. Not to get to the hardware store before it closes. But instead, I just move my body from one place to another, not to get from *point A to point B*, but to explore what is in-between: joy and innocence. The cold wind freezes my face. But my smile breaks through the ice.

The game goes on until she sprinkles a word between her laughs, a word I can't make out at first. I hear it clearly on the third yell: "Help!"

And now I'm tackled. Three men on top of my body, my body on top of the sand, the sand feeling like cement, cement feeling like it's become my Christmas carpet.

I try to explain. But when I see how happy these men are to be spending their Christmas beating on me, I realize this a mugging, not a misunderstanding. I can't fight back. My hands are held under the sand. I try to relax. I listen to the waves crashing, the silence between, and the six fists trying to coordinate who gets to break the nose, who gets to give the black eye, and who gets to give the concussion — oh yes, the season of giving. They work well together. They take turns. After all, it's Christmas. I lay here seeing stars, not sure if they are the ones in the sky or the ones in my head. I lay here feeling the pain in my jaw, not sure if it's from the punches or from smiling for the first time in ten months.

I'm not sure at what point you decide to stop punching some-one you're mugging. I'm not sure if they are tired or bored or if it's that my face is no longer the right consistency for their fists. They shake out their arms and wipe their knuckles on their jeans. The woman is behind them, looking at my bloody face like it's her masterpiece. The men take things from my pockets. They divide it amongst themselves. The woman holds out her hands and collects her payment. I can see that she thinks she deserves a bigger cut. I say that I agree. Through the blood, my words come out muffled as if spoken from a dentist chair. She giggles; and it's then that I finally hear her real laugh. The men ignore us both and leave. She looks down at me, no longer like a masterpiece but like spilled paint. "It's nothing personal," she tells me. I try to talk but my lips are numb, and I can no longer feel my tongue. She reaches her hands into my pockets. "Honey, it's nothing personal," she says again as she digs for scraps. And when there's nothing but a flattened penny I bought with two quarters, she sets it in her palm, wraps her fingers around it, turns her fist over, and throws a punch of her own. My last good eye swells up, and I can no longer see.

I imagine this is what happens next. In thirty minutes, I'll be pronounced dead. My family will get on the next flight up. My sister won't be able to wait. She'll drive through the night. When she gets here, it'll still be Christmas. She'll take a Moment to cover my corpse with a beach towel and thirty more to give a speech. The wind will toss the towel back just enough to see my feet, like a sneak peek at a gift beneath a plastic tree. And being the only person that I can trust to never grow up, she'll fulfill the contract she gifted me in a Mason jar nine Christmases ago, the one she signed with the novelty pen I wrapped in dryer sheets that same morning, the one stating that she'll do me my last favor in death. She'll turn me into a poem instead of a tombstone: *The tips of his socks looked like duck bills, flapping far past his toes.*

Green is My Favourite Colour

Todd and I lived in Ireland for eight months.

Every single night we went out to the pub.

He talked with the locals;

I skimmed through the books that lined the walls.

He came back to The States with a thick and savory Irish accent;

I came back spelling colour and favourite wrong.

~~Heads~~

Tails

so the boy waited for the train *to stop*

and he stepped ~~in front~~ inside of it.

Still curious about the other side of the quarter,

he asked the man next to him,

"What sound does it make when a train hits a human?"

"The one you'd imagine," said the man.

The boy closed his eyes and imagined it, which forced his

fingers deep into his ears. And he decided that at the next

stop — waiting for the next train — he'd spend his quarter on

a gumball.

So Then Lucas Finally Said *All Right*

So then Lucas finally said *all right.*

He threw the lemon at the car.

The car spun out and crashed into the streetlight.

The woman on the stretcher with blood coming out of her ears

would never believe that the boy tossed it underhand,

as gentle as he could,

afraid to let go.

"Honey, are you seeking appreciation from birds again?!"

Seven Hundred Miles North of Here

My seven o'clock appointment with heartbreak had become a family gathering. Everyone circled the scale in the restroom like it was a roulette wheel in the MGM. I stepped on and curled my toes toward the ground as if that might make me heavier. My family held their breath. Numbers spun into uncertainty. I awaited my evening anguish.

But on my eighth birthday, my number actually hit: 50. Right on the dot. Fifty pounds. My Dad cheered the way he did when football came back to L. A. My Mom cheered the way she always had: small jumps, big claps. My brother thrusted two fists straight into the air and cursed in victory, using his third and final *fuck ya!* my Dad allotted us every summer. My little sister's cheer was soft and shy, not for a lack of love or support, rather she just wasn't sure why any of this mattered; but she cheered anyway — like a poet trying to fit in at a Super Bowl Party. And then she hugged my hip and said, "I knew you could do it," because she could tell, for whatever reason, that it did matter. I breathed in the Moment a second longer. I held on to 50. I stayed on my podium and listened to my family's feet going down the stairs. They walked together, but I could hear them individually. I could hear my Mom's sandals slapping the wood, my Dad's slow and heavy feet taking small breaks at each step, my brother's impatient feet stuck behind Dad, and the thumps of my sister sliding down the stairs on her bottom. When the noises passed, I went to my bedroom; and I took four pounds of batteries out of my pockets.

I sat on the edge of my bed staring at a poster of Hakuhō Shō, my favorite sumo wrestler, hanging on my wall. I cried quietly (a skill I had mastered by kindergarten) until my birthday meal was ready. The meal, white rice. And what made it extra special: no sides, no veggies, no soy sauce, no meat. Just rice and chopsticks. That's how I had seen it done on TV. "Sumos eat 10,000 calories a day just in rice," I'd have to remind my Mom as I came back with my third serving. Despite being able to see my ribs through my pale skin, I was convinced sumo wrestling was my calling.

"Bones!" my Dad called up the stairs.

I pushed the tears back into my eyes with my skinny fingers and took two deep breaths.

"Bonesy!" he said even louder.

I thought about putting the batteries back in my pockets just in case later in the night they'd all want to see it again: 50. Instead, I let the missing four pounds of me be motivation to eat past the stomach pain and starchy sweat.

"Dinner's ready, Bones!" he yelled up one last time.

It was at the kitchen table that night on my eighth birthday that I vowed my nickname would one day be more ironic than descriptive. I chipped away at that life goal one bite of rice at a time. The table was already cleared and bowls were in the dishwasher when I was swallowing my last bite. I felt light-headed but my stomach felt four pounds heavier. So with that, I ran toward the scale in the restroom, this time with empty pockets. But I didn't manage to get my feet set to see the numbers. Instead, I dropped to my knees and threw up in the bathtub; and I watched my precious pounds get pulled down the drain.

Sumo wrestling never did work out. Not for a lack of will or rice, but because of an overzealous metabolism and the genetic makeup of a marathon runner — things I was told to be grateful for. In time, I took my parents' advice. I decided to be grateful; it felt a lot like giving up.

The last day of my first week of college, I sat on the small, green couch of my dorm room eating rice, a grown man weighing in at a whopping 135 pounds — no longer concerned with the scale, but still sticking to the only meal plan I ever knew, the one that gave me some sort of purpose.

Kneeling on the carpet of my dorm, Jay, my roommate, adjusted a lamp with one hand and gripped a Saint Christopher coin in the other. Jay wore a pink shirt and a red face. His beard was more gross than hip. His boots were the kind you find under a tarp in your garage, not the kind you buy with a credit card at the mall. He said things like "my goodness" and apologized after he cursed — so quickly that it sounded like a compound word: fuck-sorry.

I stared ahead at the same poster from my childhood, Hakuhō Shō in a strong sumo stance yelling "eat" in Japanese — the only motivational quote I trusted as a kid. In perfect brevity, it was the blueprint to what I wanted for my future. See, I knew exactly who I wanted to be when I was eight. But as I grew up and the dream of being a 400-pound Japanese man slipped away from me, I was overcome with uncertainty. The nebulous questions of blow-off philosophy classes, the ones that always felt like they were written by stoned teenagers in their parents' garage rather than metaphysics professors at universities, now felt like they needed new answers. Who are you? What do you want to become? Why are you still eating so much fucking rice?

Jay hit the side of the small silver lamp, hoping that old lamps work just the same as old TVs. It turned on as best it could. But this lamp couldn't light up a dog house. Jay angled it up toward the ceiling. The light barely reached the top. Half of it was still stuck to the bottom of Jay's chin. It looked like we were about to tell ghost stories.

"You've never done it?" Jay asks. "You've never prayed?"

"No, I have," I told him. "Just never asked for much."

Jay stood up, looked at his sweaty palms, wiped them on his pants, and grabbed my hands.

"Don't be nervous. It'll be fine." And then he squeezed my hands tighter. He pressed the Saint Christopher coin into my palm. "You'll need this. Go on now. It'll be fine. Close your eyes. Ask for something. Whatever you need."

I closed my eyes. It felt like I was pushed out of an airplane, and suddenly I was praying.

I prayed with my mouth, and I suppose, my soul. But my mind was on other things, much like how you can be writing a story in your head while talking to customers at checkout. I prayed with Jay in my dorm room in the forest; but I thought about my family back home, seven hundred miles south — about our nights together and how much I missed them. I thought about how Mom would sit on the edge of my bed and pray with me before I closed my eyes. My room was always Mom's first stop of three. I had, as she said, first dibs on God. I never had much to say, but I knew it was my obligation to my brother and sister to pray as long as I could. While Mom's goal was to share a small Moment in spirituality, ours was to stay awake a little longer. Prayer started at 8:30, and if we could all keep Mom in our room for ten minutes each, we'd be able to stay awake till 9:00, an hour that always felt mysterious and out of reach. (We never quite made it.)

Being a kid surrounded by love and family and good health, we didn't have much to pray for. I started by praying that the grass at school not be too wet for PE. I offered to take on the weight of all the people who prayed to lose it. And I prayed for no nightmares and, really, for no dreams at all; I prayed that when I closed my eyes all I would see is black... with little white dots. And after that, I ran into a familiar brick wall, one I'd never have enough steam to break through.

"The kid's got prayer block!" my brother and sister would joke the next morning, laughing to hide their disappointment in me not pulling my weight. I remembered all this, all these familiar memories with loved ones, while I sat in the middle of a dorm in the middle of the forest praying about something I'd never be able to recall.

I don't remember much of what I prayed for that first week of college. I remember the feeling. I remember Jay's hands and his voice guiding me. But I'm still not sure what it was that I said. But I said a lot. I prayed. And I really got on a roll. My brother and sister would have been proud, Mom, too.

"You're doing it! Now you got it," I heard Jay cheer beneath it all. "How does it feel?" he asked. "Keep this going. This is it. This is the stuff right here. I can feel it."

And then his hands gently pulled away from mine, like Dad letting go of my handlebars. "Keep going. Don't stop. Keep going," Jay said with his release. And my prayer peddled along. "Keep going. Keep going now." I kept going. Jay's voice faded into the forest. I'm not sure how long I went on. It felt like miles. My eyes had never been closed for that long while being awake. What a strange feeling that is: being awake and not seeing the things around you. Just seeing black... with little white dots.

When I finally opened my eyes, the dim light from the lamp felt much brighter.

The next morning I walked through campus for the first time without my backpack. I read the names on the plaques of all the buildings, introduced myself. I walked up stairs and down dirt paths, learned new ways around. I walked the bridge connecting campus to the city. Crossing the bridge, I looked down at the 101 and the cars passing, windshield wipers fighting for their life. In the plaza, I smiled at a man walking by me with a stack of DVDs. I took a picture of a store just called Frisbees. I joked that I'd visit it the next time I had a craving for getting an object stuck in a tree. I moved a snail from the sidewalk to a small leaf and named him Tim. I did all of this alone in a new, small town. It felt like something I'd do with my brother and sister in our old city. Except now there was no voting on what to name the snail.

Walking to school with my brother and sister we'd always see a snail on the sidewalk, apparently their natural habitat. We'd point it out. Examine it for thirty seconds. And then we'd all think of what to name it. My sister thought of names like *Miss Beauty Eyes* and *Cinderslugga*. My brother thought of names like *Slime King* and *Professor Hardback*. I pretended to be in deep thought with them, supposedly thinking up the most incredible multisyllable name. And then I'd finally offer my suggestion, trying my best to keep a serious face, trying my best not to let the giggles colonizing my gut make their way to my lips: "Tim." And then came the boos and the laughs — all blending perfectly together. "No three letter names!" my sister would protest. "It's right here in the rulebook," she'd add, pointing her finger at an imaginary rulebook in her palm.

I looked at the snail on his small leaf. And then I said goodbye to my three-lettered friend, thinking: if a snail can be a Tim, imagine who I can be. Then I found a nice bench in the center of the plaza where I sat with space between me on both sides, breathed slowly, and tried my best to remember what it was I could have been praying for.

An Overview of an Unmemorable Week of Diary Entries

A bunch of doodles of stick figures having sex, Twenty One Pilots lyrics written in yellow crayon, a reminder to take out the trash on Tuesday.

Google Scholar

Yes, you've told me (even showed me the math!) the probability of an asteroid hitting Earth on a Thursday in the year 2135, so then why is it you can't tell me the odds of a new fly coming into the house if I open the screen to let out the now fly?

Old Man

When I'm old

I want to be an old man.

You know the type,

with the old wife and the old dog.

The type who sits on a rocking chair and

falls in and out of sleep

while the rest of the house talks about things.

"It got up to ninety-five in the city today."

Those things,

you know.

But if you came up to this old man,

and if you sat across from him

and leaned in a bit

he'd tell you *other* things,

not *ninety-five in the city* things.

He'd tell you the best place to ice fish in Michigan in the winter,

which poles to bring and what beer to drink.

He'd tell you about that foul ball he caught at the World Series.

He'd tell you about the look on that child's face when he gave her the ball.

He'd tell you that you gotta hike the John Muir Trail before you get too old.

He'd tell you this

and tell you that

if you just went over there

and leaned in a bit.

I want to be *that* old man.

The one in the rocking chair falling in and out of sleep,

with lots of things to say,

but not saying a word...

because everyone just leaves him

alone.

Food Fight

Although the first rebellious whispers came from the bravest lips, and though the populace of the playground supported the war, and even with the cafeteria supplying the bullets, the first shot was never fired — and the lunch attendants, who caught wind of the rumor earlier that day, would often wonder if the peace that lunch period came from a sudden sensibleness or if it was just a corollary of what was on the cafeteria menu: how is it that you would throw tomato bisque?

Facts: According to the Laws of Pervasive Slapstick Comedy

▸ The average American will slip on four banana peels a day.

▸ It's impossible to discern the front from the back of a bottle of pepper spray.

▸ The scent of pie has antigravity effects.

▸ Admiration is won with a match and a fart.

▸ Comedy clubs put a whole tomato under each patron's seat.

▸ There's a better chance a grand piano falls on your head than a raindrop.

▸ Hugs evolved from a basic human need to put a "kick me" sign on someone's back.

▸ The most efficient way to dismount a horse is to not see that branch coming.

The MFA Student

"I don't know why I can't write a story. I've read McKee's *Story*. I've read Stephen King's *On Writing*. I've read Snyder's *Save The Cat* and I've read Field's *The Foundation*."

"Have you tried sitting down and writing?"

"Who's that by?"

A Smart Mother

Mother made the kids fart in the *fart corner*. It kept the kids polite.

Mother made the *fart corner* the same corner as the *timeout corner*. It kept the kids well-behaved.

Mechanic Milking a Cow

Thanksgiving

I don't eat meat, but I still cut the turkey. It's Thanksgiving morning
and things need to get done. There's no time to question the roles
Dad assigned to us nineteen years ago, no room for my ethics in the
kitchen. Dad directs the culinary chaos. Points to things. Moves things
from the fridge to the counter, from the counter to the oven. Hands
us stuff. Hands my sister the sweet potatoes and the potato peeler.
Hands my brother the white potatoes and the masher. Hands my
Mom the butter and the measuring spoons. And he hands me the
turkey; and he hands me the knife, the one that most resembles
a chainsaw.

It's not that he's trying to be cruel to me. It's just that he doesn't
understand it much. He can't see how those two things might inter-
fere with each other: me not eating animals, and me having to cut a
turkey with a serrated-electric-carving-knife. He might not compre-
hend my compassion, but he respects my values. He has a corner of
the kitchen designated for my diet. When it's time to eat, he'll make
sure no one takes my tofurky. And he'll be so excited to ask me how
it tastes.

"Did I do good?" he'll want to know.

"It's perfect," I'll tell him.

But first, I have to slay an already slaughtered bird. I have to cut
the turkey. I have to do my job.

My little sister tries to comfort me, says, "No feathers at least."
And I say, "You're right." But I still see the feathers. I see the beak,

the eyes, those silly feet, that funny neck. I hear the chirps and the gobbles. And then, of course, the shrieks. The loud, loud shrieks.

But the knife is loud, too; and it's for that — each year — I'm most thankful.

Amy

There's a naked picture of myself in a pink envelope in my pocket.
And there's good reason to send it to an eighth grader in New Jersey.

She's my most difficult pen pal. Her letters to me always have a
muddy handprint wrapped around the envelope. When I asked her
about this, she said, "Mailmen in your area must have dirty hands."
She puts letters to paper like a knife to a tree. I can see the spots
where her pencil brakes — most often in the middle of words like
shithead or *dickhead* or any other word she uses to describe her Dad.
She must go through a pack of pencils when she's writing of her father.
She says she's not scared to say all this to his face, but he's deaf
in one ear, and instead of turning the good ear toward her, he says,
"Walk around" — and when she does, he says, "Not in front of the TV."
It's just easier she do her complaining on paper.

Her letters are my least favorite to read. She doesn't ask much
about me, only sometimes asking if she could see me naked or if I
could send her gift cards to Macy's. But she writes me twice a month,
and in that regard she's worth double my other pen pals; and her
name is Amy, which makes her worth incalculable.

She signs her name just how I beg her to, with the *A* slanted
gently to the right, and the M with no sharp points, and the Y sinking
off the paper and then swooping back up — just how I'd seen it writ-
ten all over my house for all my twelve years. Walking from kitchen to
bathroom to living room to garage with the phone jammed between
her shoulder and ear, my Mom would write her name on anything

that would take ink while talking to my Dad as he drove home from work. On the days when Dad drove fast, Mom would only need the backs of old newspaper and a few stacks of sticky notes. With Dad in gridlock, Mom would have to expand her canvas, writing her name on anything from toilet paper to old orange peels.

Her name was everywhere. All over everything in the house. It was impossible not to read it when walking by, but as my brain sounded out those three letters, all I ever heard was *Mom*. I can still hear it now.

It took two years for any of us to admit that there would be no more new notes to discover floating around the house. And it took us another two years to finally clean up.

"What do you think Dad hears?" my sister asks me with a handful of sticky notes covered in Mom. "Just put them in," I tell her, nodding toward the paper-filled cardboard box, the one that an hour earlier housed our plastic Christmas tree. Now it holds what might as well be Mom's ashes. "Ready?" Dad asks, bent down next to the box. We nod, even though we know the question is really for himself.

Dad is bent down on one side of the box, me and my sister on the other. He stretches his arms so that one is on each end, and now it's as if there are two people on each side of the carry — how it used to be, the days when Mom and Dad used to say to me and my sister, "Wouldn't life be a bore if we didn't have four?"

One, two, three, lift.

It's lighter than it was with the Christmas tree, but it's hard to carry in its own way. It's a new path for all of us. Instead of carrying the box from the living room back to the garage — where we always store it after setting up the tree — we carry it up the stairs and down the thin hall and into the dark office. We set it by the paper shredder, and we sit on the floor. This is the real funeral, Dad says.

For hours we shred sticky notes, newspapers, envelopes, every bit of Mom — until the box is empty, and the shredder is full.

We pull the bin from the shredder and look into it like a casket.

My sister says that paper shreds are used as bedding for composting worms and that composting worms' castings are great for soil. We can start a garden, she says. "Let's start a garden," she says, now reaching deep into the bin of shredded paper with one arm, playing with it between her fingers. And now we all have an arm buried in the bin, and we let our hands move however they might move. "Maybe," Dad says. "Or maybe we just glue them back together."

With my other arm I feel around in my pocket. I feel the pink envelope and the picture inside of it: my naked twelve-year-old frame standing in front of a dirty mirror, my blurry body from my shaky hands, the sweat on my forehead, the strange smirk (*Don't smile*, she instructed), the red on my face, the white everywhere else — my monthly subscription to a freshly inked *Amy*.

Some Stuff

Enlightenment
I don't need to smoke weed to enjoy myself. I just need a few close friends…
to hotbox whatever room I'm in.

Singing
I'm so bad at singing I spelled Mississippi wrong.

Air Instruments
Playing air piano looks a lot like playing someone else's air bass.

Black and White
I learned that dogs only see black and white… so I painted my cat purple.

If I
If I was the last person on earth, who would propose this hypothetical?

Midnight Walks
Ever since I got a dog, my midnight walks feel a lot less suspicious.

Keep the Dialogue Rolling
Popular dieticians have this strategy to easily keep their weight in check even when eating fast food. At the drive-thru, they like to exclude one item of food from their order to reduce their caloric intake.

I like to exclude one item from my order so when they ask, "Anything else?" I can keep the dialogue rolling.

Popular Science
Harvard Research Team discovers that lab mice given small doses of marijuana are way more popular than sober mice.

Some More Stuff

Genie

If a genie came out of a lamp and granted me three wishes,
I'd ask for a new lamp.

College

School doesn't prepare you for real life, it prepares you for more
school. There has to be a solution to this flaw in the education
system… but I'm scared it's more school.

The best thing I've seen at an open mic:

A bald man in his eighties played the entire *Shrek* soundtrack and
then left. He didn't once acknowledge that he was only playing songs
from *Shrek*. It was amazing.

Metaphysics and Cab Rides

I asked our cab driver if he knew where he was going, and he said,
"Just because I think I know where I'm going, doesn't mean I know
where I'm going." And I said, "You're a better philosopher than a
cab driver."

Rejected *Most Interesting Man In The World* Joke:

When he farts in the car, passengers scramble to roll their windows *up*.

An Artist Stuck in Room 301

Don't underestimate the kid in fifth grade

who asks if he can borrow a pencil,

who doesn't know what page the teacher is reading from,

who still has water on the collar of his shirt from the drinking fountain,

who has dirty shorts from sitting on the blacktop reading comics,

who doesn't care much about anything he's supposed to care about,

the kid who stuffs all his papers into his backpack,

no folder, no binder, no spiral notebook,

just a bunch of paper in a backpack.

He's not doing great right now.

But he's on to something.

Elizabeth Lizzy Beth

The combo was easy, *7-right 11-left 17-right*. My Dad made it hard, "Just remember they are all prime numbers." I fumbled my fingers around the dial while the bell rang for reading comprehension — a class where you hoped you didn't get called on to read, and you prayed that stuttering Keith didn't get called on to read (tolerance and acceptance for those with speech impediments wasn't taught until the following semester). You always got called on to read. Keith soon followed. My brain played Tetris with all the prime numbers, and I eventually got my locker to cooperate with my pulls.

Miss Prater was probably midway through roll call, laboriously trying to pronounce the three-letter first names of the consistent handful of Nguyens. I carried my stack of books, having been told backpack kids are the worst type of kids. I could barely see; I might as well have been carrying around an air-conditioning unit, stumbling the halls looking for the class I would later be able to walk to blindfolded and brainwashed. At this point Miss Prater was probably moving onto the O's, where Ben Oats (the least popular kid in school due to an early awareness of his atheism) would nod his head as a slick sub-stitute for speech. The halls were empty with the exception of myself and another lost student and an awkwardly worded "*Well, Welcome New Students*" sign that hung over the somehow already sticky lunch tables. I later found out the disoriented girl's name was Elizabeth, but she liked to be called Lizzy, but everyone just called her Beth — the nickname had more to do with disrespect than a collective liking for brevity. Lizzy already had her braces off, which was enough to make her one of the most noteworthy girls in school. Maybe she never even had braces, but she stood with the confidence of someone who had just gotten them off. Her hair looked soft. If I shaped my hand into scissors I imagine I could cut right through it. Her blonde hair was unbridled, shining some insight on her social standing. With hair like that, she couldn't have been one of those sixth graders that participated in the eight-girl braiding trains that went on fifteen minutes before school started. I like to think she spent that time reading the same comics I liked to read.

At this point, Miss Prater was likely toward the end of roll call. The Thompson twins were probably giggling as they switched first names for the day, and Zach was probably telling the teacher he wanted to be called Zachary, feeling the shorthand wouldn't match his dress socks.

Lizzy's eyes squinted, fixing in on her discovered destination. She walked faster than she could have jogged — a pace that told me she had no idea the insignificance of being late on the first day or how ridiculous power walking in a long denim skirt looked. Suddenly, as if someone had stuck their leg out in front of her, she tripped. Her books took flight in all the wrong directions. Her arms flailed away from her body like they were under the influence of a drunk puppeteer.

Her calculator beat her to the floor, a cruel foreshadowing of her fate. It slid across the ground until it shattered against the wall. Her elbows greeted the floor with a heavy punch. Her hips followed. The right side of her face finalized her fall. She laid there, shifting around as if in a painful sleep.

I ducked behind a block of rusted lockers. I ignored her fall. I let her pick herself up. I let her gather her books. I let her knees bleed and her hips bruise.

The way I saw it, I saved her that day. A helping hand in that Moment would have been temporary aid. But it would give life to the memory. She'd know that I saw it all. When we do awful things alone, we can bury them behind better memories. So I let her have her Moment; and I let her forget about it. I let a few minutes pass, emerged from the lockers, and entered class carrying an unfamiliar guilt of being late.

Inspired by valueless bonus points that would at best amount to a handful of expired Almond Joys, the classroom had life. I looked three desks to my left and noticed Beth. She sat nervously as she stared at a blank page. Her already bruised wrists dangled pencil-less by her side. The boy next to her had a zebra striped pencil bag on his desk spilling over with spare erasers and pens. But the bag was invisible to Beth. She couldn't collect the courage to ask him to borrow one. She couldn't do it. She looked like she had braces now. Maybe she didn't read comics with those precious minutes before the bell rang; maybe she was just at the back of the braiding train. The fall bruised her body with uncertainty. She started crying and left the classroom.

My pencil slipped from my hand and dropped on the floor. I tried the slouch-in-your-desk-and-reach-your-leg-out trick, but it was too far even for my disproportionly long bottom limbs. I crawled onto all fours and picked it up. I walked over to Lizzy's desk and set it down and whispered sorry to an empty seat as if setting a flower on a grave. I immediately regretted my theatrics as one of the four Matts jokingly jabbed, "It's ok, buttercup," and high-fived some other Matt to publicize his Moment of classroom wit.

Seven long class periods later, I woke up from a sleepless stare at the inside of my elbow. Our teacher was drawing a picture to go along with that annoying *two trains* leave the station word problem that overstates the ubiquity of twenty-first century train travel. After the train discussion had gone a predicted nowhere, our teacher ended class with a first-day-of-school survey. The first six questions were told to be answered with a Yes or No. The last question demanded a little more.

7) How was your first day of sixth grade? (Explain)

I read it three times before answering.

How was your first day of sixth grade?
How was it?
How was your day?

When the final bell rang and the day was officially over, the soccer field turned into a beach. Everyone gathered in groups and created separate circles connected by equal popularity. The most prestigious circle looked like an oval. Half the kids leaned back onto their forearms and elbows while the others rocked back and forth from their tailbones, wrapping their knees to their chest. The less capable circle settled for a square. Each differently-shaped circle slowly disconnected as parents' cars pulled up to the gate, until it was just Lizzy and me. I turned and faced her, making our circle a straight line. She kept her head down and picked at the grass.

"Hey," I said, but should have yelled.

"What?" She yelled, overcompensating for the distance between us.

I smiled.

"Hey," she said at perfect volume.

A silence that I was unprepared for blanketed the grass. I got up and walked toward her. I realized that walking would extend the silence even further, so I ran. Having played enough third person video games to visualize my situation from a bird's-eye view, I saw how disconcerting running full speed at a girl picking grass looked, so I eased up into a confusing jog that looked more like a masculine skip.

I stopped and sat down a few feet in front of her.

"I'm Darren."

She looked up, pretending that she hadn't seen my confusing journey over.

"I'm Lizzy."

"I know."

"You like Bob Dylan?"

"Who?"

"Bob Dylan."

"Ya. Wait, who?"

I looked down and remembered I was wearing my brother's Bob Dylan shirt (because it was green, not because I had an early appreciation for lyrically groundbreaking folk music). I lied, "Ya, I like him a lot."

Then she asked, "What's your favorite song of his?"

I tried to guide the conversation in a direction less demanding of my knowledge of music.

"Oh, hey, what did you get for number seven?" I asked.

"You know those aren't graded, right?"

"Just curious what you put."

I was aware of my voice and how I was talking and how I was listening. I hadn't talked all day. I'm sure she hadn't either. But now we were, and it felt good.

She looked past my shoulder to acknowledge and ignore the first honk from her ride. She went to answer my question before being interrupted by another string of honks. It got her to her feet and running. Halfway to her Mom's car, she turned around and yelled across the field to me. She didn't yell loud enough. I'm pretty sure she said, "I think I got number seven wrong." Or maybe she said, "How do you not know one Bob Dylan song?"

Definitions

Basketball shoes: worn while playing basketball.

Running shoes: worn while running.

Rock climbing shoes: worn while rock climbing.

Tennis shoes: worn while sitting on the asphalt of your old high school drinking two forties behind the handball wall across from the tennis courts.

More Definitions

Camping: formally known as living.
Humans: animals wearing hats.

The Bachelor: Polygamy Addition

Eighteen girls will fight for love

Two or three will go home heartbroken

Things that Can Be Seen From Space

a. The Great Pyramid of Giza.

b. The Great Wall of China.

c. The guy in the car that doesn't know his high beams are on.

d. A cloud of smoke coming from The Gospel Swamp concert.

e. A yellow truck double-parked in a liquor store parking lot.

f. That monster set wave everyone just fake paddled for.

g. The line at the grocery store because for some reason 13 of the 14 registers are always closed.

h. That guy at that rave doing that thing with the glow sticks.

i. A floral couch on the curb with a *free* sign on it.

j. A stack of unfinished listicles on an author's desk.

k.

l.

m.

n.

o.

p.

q.

r.

s.

t.

u.

v.

w.

x.

y.

z.

Diary Entry #621

From a bumby plane ride across the
Pacific, to a gentle, early morning landing
in Southeast Asia (Bangkok, to be exact). We
took a van to Chiang Mai — jet lagged
and ~~this~~ whiskey-less. If there were a
day for tired eyes and sobriety it was
today. The city had enough energy already.
A pep in my step would have been like
a caffeine pill in a coffee. I took
a deep breath and crossed the road
and ate the ~~food~~: a meat that was
new to me. I considered each bite.
I walked and smiled, took photos and
mingled, stood still and listened. Locals
yelled and talked fast; I replayed
their words slowly in my head, not with
the intention to understand them better,
but just to hear them again. Stray
dogs and stray cats walked and laid.
Children sped in and out ~~of traffic~~
on their scooters to school. A cat
licked its paws. A ~~scoot~~ scooter came
toward it.

I've seen
you do this
before
hahaha

At ~~least~~ the last second the cat launched itself out of the way. It sat in its new spot and went back to licking its paws until the next scooter came. Things moved both fast and slow in Chiang Mai. I kept chewing, considering each bite — everything new to me.

T.S

Diary Entry #622

Wish I didn't eat that meat yesterday.
So sick. Pooping. Throwing up. Sweating.
Everything hurts. I wanna go home.

T.S

hahahaha

I Asked You Three Questions

"What's your favorite candy? Whiskey or Wine? Are you afraid of heights?"

That night, I knocked on your door holding a bag of Jolly Ranchers and a bottle of Merlot. We took a drive to the sea, where we laid a blanket atop a grassy cliff that served as front row seats to the sunset. I was nervous that you thought it would be too much, or not enough — and those nerves kept me quiet and scared.

The sounds of the seals and the salty smell of the ocean climbed the cliff and ran up our bodies. The grass grew through the blanket, tickling our backs. Our feet flirted with the empty space that led down to the ocean. The dolphins played with the waves and the clouds moved across the moon. The stars won the war against city lights and fog. The world around us was doing its part. It was my turn to participate, to shake the silence, to give you the date I dreamed of giving you.

I opened the bottle of wine and things began to move.

The first swig led to the first Jolly Rancher. We blindly grabbed one from the bag. There was purple in our palms and disgust on our face.

"What are the odds," I said. And then I threw my medicine flavored candy up toward the moon and down into the ocean.

"I never took stats," you said. And then you threw your medicine-flavored candy up toward Mars and down into the ocean. "But I did play base-ball," you joked.

Things continued to move.

I told you I wish you answered whiskey; you told me we probably just killed two fish. Your sweaty hands told me you actually *were* afraid of heights; my hands told you that I wouldn't let you fall.

And as the night moved around us and we moved with it, we kept feeding the Pacific with purple Jolly Ranchers — occasionally justifying our pollution with spurious statistics about symbiotic relationships between ecosystems and sugary snacks. We were being silly. Two people being silly, the first step to two people being serious.

And we lay there chatting and laughing until we both decided we were too drunk to be falling in love that close to the edge of a cliff.

@_ _nitch

"It's fun to read quotes by famous people, isn't it? It's fun to pretend that there's a special breed of humans out there who don't waste words. Have you read Bruce Lee quotes? No words wasted. They'd have me convinced he's never asked the waitress where the bathroom is. But listen, I'm sure he has. He could've bitten his tongue and just looked around, found the signs and figured it out. How hard can it be? It's usually in the corner. But even Bruce Lee has asked the waitress where the bathroom is. Do you know what I mean by all this? To be quoted isn't to be voiced, but to be edited down to intellectual certitude. And that's the highest honor. Why? I could explain in great detail, but I've already said too much. Please, only use those first two sentences. Hack away at the unessential. I think Bruce Lee said that."

–Toddy Smith

No One Wants to go Bowling

When you're desperate, you can find yourself in a musky alley wearing shoes that don't fit because you don't want to bother the man behind the counter a second time. You'll find yourself with your fingers stuffed inside a heavy, green ball, staring down some pins, trying to convince yourself it's a great game to play on an evening like this, trying to think it up as a good night, a nice outing, some sort of fun time. And when you go into work at the beginning of the week and your co-workers ask you about your weekend, you try to think of something to tell them, you try to whip something up, tell them about something you did, anything, anything but bowling.

Higher Places

You know *the nod*. Two guys walk past each other both wearing Raiders hats; they give the nod. A surfer recognizes another surfer, and he gives her the nod. The Jeep Wrangler drives past the Jeep Wrangler — nod, nod.

I'm on the curb of 8th and G smoking an old cigarette and twirling a pen, trying to think of something to write. The homeless man who poops on the sidewalk gives me the nod. The woman who pretends to be a scarecrow in the plaza gives me the nod. The local bike thief gives me the nod. I nod, and I keep trying to think of something to write. If it's good enough, maybe my nods will come from higher places: from a man sipping espresso on the balcony of his overpriced apartment in Los Angeles, from a poet reading from her chapbook on stage at a university, from people with friends who call them from time to time.

Diary Entry # 801

We traveled the north island in a
shaky RV, passing more sheep than cars
and stopping when someone saw a sight
they wanted to touch: a waterfall, a
green field that went on like the ocean,
or even just an unfamiliar road sign
we didn't have back in the states.
~~[scribbled out]~~
~~[scribbled out]~~

In the RV, we shared chocolate
bars and boy talk. In the RV, old
soup cans served as barf bags
and bets were placed on who would
yack first. Days on the road blended
together. I'd go to take a bite of my
candy bar to realize I finished it
three bites ago. I'd say a joke in
my best New Zealand accent and
be reminded that I did that bit
eighty miles ago. Someone would barf
and I'd ~~think~~ think I won the bet,
~~forgetting~~ I called the first soup can
into service at yesterday's nauseating

183

Dude, this sentence is perfect.

Mountain pass. The road brought everything ~~together~~ together— the people, the time, ~~thoughts~~ — and it blended them into a pot of surreal experience, and it felt like, despite being in a shaky RV in the middle of nowhere, well, it felt like we were a part of everything, moving with uncertainty with everyone else who had ever moved with uncertainty. And soon enough the trip was done, and I was back at home driving on smooth roads in a small car, driving past things that I'd never touched, only stopping when the light turned red or I got to where I had to be.

T.S

Diary Entry #802

Mom seems upset that I didn't get her
a souvenir. Dad seems to have no idea
that I was in a different country for
the past three weeks.

| T.S

hahahaha

glad you're
back.

Man Deciding if He Wants to Lose His Money Systematically or All at Once

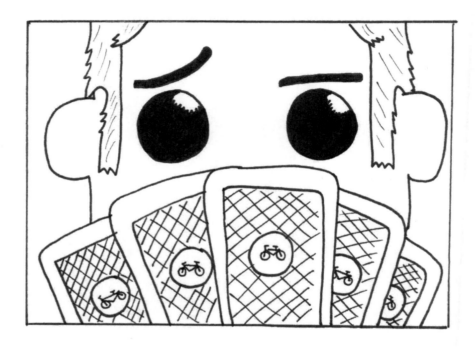

A Long Drive Home

Red 16 and I'll go home with a fuzzy whale for my niece and two months' rent. Anything else and I'll be lucky to make it home at all. My stomach will hurt until the ball stops spinning. And when it lands, there's a good chance it'll hurt even more. And when I ask the sweet woman filling her tank at the gas station for a few dollars, it'll hurt the most.

First Day of School

I got my daughter ready for her first day of school. She put her small foot on my knee, and I tied her shoes tight. She tucked her chin down toward her Minnie Mouse t-shirt, and I straightened the white bow in her brown hair. She turned her back toward me and I zipped all the zippers on her purple backpack. She extended one arm out and then the other, and I slipped her into her bulletproof vest.

I Wish It Hurt Like It Used To

Another one, Texas this time. I'm in California and no one is crying.
My sister suggests we change the channel how she does when an old
episode of *Sanjay and Craig* comes on: re-run! seen it! this one again?

A news anchor asks for our *Thoughts and Prayers*.
But my thoughts are more about myself: is there such a thing as a
bulletproof helmet? And my prayers are more about the location of
the clicker: what cushion is it under this time?

Something happened in Texas. I'm somewhere else.
In some *state* where the demand is no longer for change in policy,
but for someone to just please change the channel.

Stories from The Beach/ Stories from Home

9

I make the sand into a hospital bed and admit myself. A stingray has swelled my foot two sizes up. I tell my brother to pee on it. It's not science, but it's a respected myth in these parts. My brother approaches, first making a joke, squatting over my foot, squeezing and grunting like he misunderstands the protocol. *"Number one, not two!"* I yell. He drops his trunks lower than he needs to, lets it hang however it falls, pees on more than just my foot.

At home I ask my brother why his is bigger if I am older. He says be patient. "One day you'll learn to get over it."

13

My Mom sees a dolphin. I squint my eyes and try to follow the line of her finger out to sea. I have no chance. Her finger is small and shaky. The ocean is big and still. My eyes are the worst in the family. I pretend I catch a glimpse of the fin: "Beautiful."

At home I tell Dad all about the dolphin I pretended to see. He asks me about the blowhole, and I say it was the best blowhole I've ever seen. Joel Osteen is on the TV during dinner, telling me the fate of a liar. I lean in and listen. By the second commercial, my pork chops are too cold to eat. "No dinner, no dessert," Dad says, grabbing ice-cream bowls for everyone but me.

15

Under the pier, I ask my date if she can take me home now. She says no, a plane just crashed on the highway. I say, "Which lane?"

At home I tell her she can't come in. She tells me she'll tip-toe. I tell her I don't like her like that. She tells the tenth grade that I have a poster of Clay Aiken above my bed.

19

There's a chew toy in the sand, a rubber chicken leg sitting in front of the sunset. My dog's health tells her to ignore it. She stays in my lap. She's too sick to even leave the house — this is what I'm told. But if I tug on her collar hard enough, she'll follow me anywhere. See, we're both sick in our own ways.

At home I have the mailman stand at the front window. Keep him there two whole minutes. Use him like smelling salts. But my dog just keeps staring, motionless. I try to remind her how to do it. I bark at the poor guy. Paw at his chest. Knock a few envelopes from his bag. Still, nothing.

I read an essay arguing against euthanasia. I take notes. Memorize the key points. Run a brush through her hair and tell her she'll live forever.

23

A bottle of whiskey sticks out from the sand like an umbrella. It's not mine. It's not empty. It's not my best Moment.

At home I scrub my lips with a cotton ball soaked in mouthwash. I call a number my Mom has given me on three separate occasions, written each time on the back of a family photo. Check-in is early the next morning. They will send someone to pick me up, to help with the transition (also probably has something to do with their treatment center having no place to park my car for six weeks). I sleep in till noon, ignore the doorbell, the loud knocks, and the sweet woman's voice just trying to help.

27

On the lifeguard tower I hold out my arms like Moses and part the Pacific Ocean so the children can walk to Catalina Island and play with the bison.

At home my girlfriend doesn't believe in psychotic breakdowns, says I probably just ate something rotten. Tells me to drink a glass of water and go to bed.

31

At the end of the pier, behind the diner that makes the cranberry sauce my Dad likes so much, I decide the best way to jump would be head first. Rocks fill my pockets; my ex-girlfriend's ankle weights cuff my jeans. I see a good spot to jump, near a fishing boat with four strong men, one of them telling stories of the Navy, a cigar and a stingray in his left hand.

At home I'm on the six o'clock news as *Man Saved by US Veteran*. The phone rings. My manuscript suddenly gains traction; these stories suddenly make perfect sense. Let's just edit out this one part, they tell me: the part with the fishing boat, the four strong men, one of them telling stories of the Navy...

But this, they should know, is my favorite part.

Why Are the Writers So Sad?

a. They see someone using their book as a coaster.

b. They bought into the misconception that writers have to be miserable if they want to be taken seriously.

c. They understand that only .00001% of people make valuable contributions to their field while the majority of creatives simply keep the field afloat so when someone more creative than them comes around that more creative person will have enough reference material to use as stepping stones toward something revolutionary — something truly Creative.

d. They fear their art won't make you happy. (They hope you're happy.)

Those Buggy Eyes

It always went this way: after an hour of solo surfing, my Dad paddles in (doesn't say anything about the impressive mounds of sand I invested my morning in), drags me across my habitat and into his, lays me on his yellow longboard and pushes it past the break toward the horizon like a Norse funeral, and he smiles like it was a wedding; and I give in, too scared to object to my arranged marriage to the sea, too scared that if I didn't paddle out with him, he'd have no reason to ever paddle back in.

I just liked to push sand into mounds with my hands while I watched him surf before school. But he had a plan to fix me up, to make me a sea creature like him. I had to catch six waves before he'd take me to school (or rather, a few blocks shy from school — his decision not mine). Six waves every day. By my tenth birthday I'd be at four hundred thirty-eight waves. And if he upped my dose to ten waves a day — an idea he flirted with as if it was experimental medicine — I'd be well over a thousand in no time. "In no time, you'll shake your land legs and be a sea-creature like me."

Some kids are scared their parents will make them move to a new school in Texas; I was scared my Dad would make us live in the ocean. And I remember that first day when I thought maybe my Dad would have been better off if we did.

Empty waters. The sea was a lake — a day where a real surfer checks the surf report, says *it's shit*, and goes home to clean the garage instead.

My first wave came when school started. Wave three came an hour later, about the time when the kids on land were going over last night's homework. Wave five came around 10:00 a.m., about that time when the kids on land were quietly reading before recess. That penultimate wave took me to shore (what a tease). I gripped the ocean floor between my toes. Then I released. And I made the trek back out for number six on that yellow longboard — that ten-foot piece of fiberglass that shuttled me back and forth between two worlds. I paddled out, each pull of water pushing me further from home. My Dad was treading water with his hands up in the air, fists pumping, celebrating my fifth wave of my two hundred ninety-second straight day of surfing the same way someone would celebrate the first wave of their life. It wasn't so much that I was paddling out, it was more that he was pulling me in.

The calm continued. The distance between five and six was always greater than any two numbers. It was as if we were in an abandoned wave pool waiting for someone to buy it, sign the papers, clean it up, hire a crew, and get it back in business. I sat on the yellow long-board just how my Dad taught me to sit on it, not crisscrossed like my instincts told me to. My legs dangled in the ocean, which scared me. My Dad's whole body was in there, which scared me more.

And then I asked him: "Aren't you afraid?"

"Of what?" he asked. And then he looked out toward Catalina, eyeing a wave moving in like a sound sitting atop a toddler's tongue.

"Sharks. Stingrays. Jellies?"

"Turn," he said.

In time my small body turned the big board to shore. He held onto the back, ready to push me into it. "Paddle." I paddled. He pushed me forward, thrusting me into the wave toward the shore. But he didn't let go. He pulled me back. "Nope. Not this one. Not big enough," he said.

▶▶

I didn't think it was a time to be picky. I remember wanting to say just that. Instead, I stayed silent and watched wave number six crumble atop the shore, taunting me.

"Nice out. Isn't it, bud?" my Dad asked.

"Sure."

"This is cool, huh?"

I didn't respond. I put it on him to explain to me how being stranded at sea was cool.

"Me, an adult, out here on a Tuesday. You, a kid, out here on a Tuesday. Two boys on the lam."

"The lamb?"

"The lam. The run. It's an old man's term."

And then he sunk to the bottom of the ocean floor and shot back up like he was on a pogo stick. He shook his hair like a dog. He didn't rub his eyes like I had to do after coming up from the salt water. And he didn't gasp for air — it was as if there wasn't anything above water that he couldn't get beneath it.

"On the lam in the ocean," he said.

And we both laughed: me at the image of a lamb in the ocean, my Dad at the sad truth of his statement.

It was then that I understood all the waves he let pass. To me, they were a bus home. To him, it was the bullet train to hell. He prescribed me medicine so he could take it. The more time I spent on the board, the more time he spent off of it — buried in saltwater, hiding most of himself, as close to disappearing as he could get. He always kept himself strategically submerged. If his mouth and nose were on the top of his head, I would have never seen his eyes.

I tried again: "Dad, aren't you afraid?"

"Of what?" he asked again.

"Sharks. Stingrays. Jellies?"

My Dad floated closer to me and began picking at the wax on the board with his fingernails.

"I'm more concerned with the little fish," he said. "Those buggy eyes. The way they look at you."

Then he sank to the bottom of the ocean. And this time I thought he'd never come up. And when he finally did, he was cupping his hands together holding something tight. He brought his clasped hands toward my body and then released them. Sand poured out onto the yellow board. I brought my legs out of the water and crossed them neatly, and we pushed the sand around into small mounds as if we were sitting on the shore. And we kept playing with it until he finally decided that the ocean fell asleep on us.

I paddled in. He swam next to me. I got to school at the very end of recess, where the rules of sports are evaporated by impatience and everything turns to jungle ball — free and wild, no rules, no worries. Dad went home, where there was a bathtub too small to sink into. I thought about all this on the playground. About how my Dad insists he drop me off three blocks from school. About how he only grocery shops at night. About how he wears his long jacket and hood even in the summer. About his article in *The New York Times* criticizing the invention of the mirror. About his favorite story in the *Paris Review* about Blanchot being photographed only three times. About how there were no cameras in our house. About my grounding when I pointed one from school in his direction. About the sharks, stingrays, and jellies being nothing in comparison to those buggy eyes.

Now, I'm out here at sea (escaping the one thing on land no one can run from) on the thick yellow board with remnants of the same wax from fifteen years ago; and I know he'd be proud of his son, a sea creature when he needed to be — a man on the lam in the ocean.

A wave comes and I let it pass.

Tears come and I let them pour.

At home, his wetsuit still hangs in the front yard like a windchime, the puddle beneath it begins to dry out. In the morning, the small birds will have to find a new bath for their feet.

The waves come and it's easy now to let them pass.

Juice Box

I'm drinking juice like a "kid," but I'm reading the nutrition facts like a man. And now I know that the first ingredient in cranberry juice is apple juice. Interesting, right? I can't help but think this can be related to the world somehow. *Things aren't always as they seem* or *truths are diluted with falsehoods.* Cranberry juice is a metaphor of sorts. Cranberry juice is philosophy. I'm really onto something! This is deeper than you'd ever know! A twenty-six-year-old man drinking a juice box in his underwear at 11:00 a.m. isn't childish! Can't you see I'm on a metaphysical voyage, Mom?!

A Chicken in a Lemon Tree

The neighbor's chicken snuck into the backyard again. It climbed my lemon tree and tested the top branch. The weight of curiosity sank it low. The chicken hurried toward the edge of the branch as if the leaf at the tip — ready to be taken by the wind — was the bus about to drive off. And when the leaf blew away, the chicken waited at the edge, not knowing where to go from here.

I asked my Dad if I should call 911.

"That's only for cats," he told me. "Just go catch 'em," he said as he walked out the front door for work.

So I walked out back and held out my arms and looked up. The chicken just stared down at me, shaking the weak branch, making it look like a rubber pencil. The wind picked up and it started to rain. I stayed out back for an hour with my arms extended, stiff and ready to catch. I imagine I looked silly — like I was holding an invisible cardboard box. But I imagine I looked even worse when my arms got tired and I went back inside and called 911 regarding a chicken in a lemon tree.

The Most Important Thing

"Don't just fall in love with someone… fall in love with life *with someone*."

"Shut up, Kyle. You're stoned."

Lycidas

A year ago I had to read Milton's *Lycidas*. I bought a used copy of *Milton's Complete Collection of Poems* buried in the back of an old bookshop. It was stained, ripped, and bent. The previous owner seemingly shared the same negative attitude I had toward Milton's work. Every stanza was stuffed with pessimistic annotations:

Eww/Boring/Horrible

But the final sentence, "Tomorrow to fresh woods, and pastures new," was highlighted in yellow and underlined in bright purple. It was circled in red pen and was surrounded by happy faces and sloppy hearts. I fell in love with the sentence as deeply as the previous reader must have. This one sentence must have spoken to him or her, and surely it spoke to me.

I flipped to the front page to try and find the owner's name. I needed to know who shared the same consistent distaste for 192 lines of Milton's acclaimed pastoral eulogy as me. And I needed to know the name of the person who was, just as I was, converted on the 193rd line.

On the front cover was the name *Mary L* in faded pencil.

After a series of questionable breaches of privacy, I found her phone number and sent her a text: "Tomorrow to fresh woods, and pastures new."

My phone vibrated: "Umm, what?"

I explained to her how I found joy in that quote, just like she did. Then I received a lengthy train of alternating H's and A's followed by an explanation:

"No, I just love the Last Sentence of every poem... because it means that the poem is finally over."

I flipped through the collection of poems and sure enough every Last Sentence of every poem was lit up with highlighter and under-lined in bright colors and hearts.

I was fascinated. I asked her if she was free.

At the end of the pier I reached into my pocket and pulled out a stack of the Last Sentences from the book that was once hers. We alternated reading them out loud. And after each one was read, we tossed it in the garbage can full of old fishing line and empty beer cans. And when the last *Last Sentence* was read, we leaned on the rail of the pier and just stared out to sea and let the waves and the birds and the seals fill the silence as they pleased.

It was mostly quiet, and that was okay. She was right — whether she just hated poetry or understood it beyond traditional analysis — words are best when they can find a place to end.

The One About the Girl Who Placed Last in the Spelling Bee

First you were an author, and now you are a babysitter. Your brother-in-law says you're going backwards with your career. You tell him you're going alphabetically.

He and your sister are on their way out to see a movie that started fifteen minutes ago. But they don't rush. The first thing you learn as a parent is how to be late.

Your sister has the movie tickets on her cellphone. Your brother-in-law says he misses the good old days with real tickets. (When you become a father it's easy to forget you're still a Millennial.)

What movie, you ask. He says the one with Kevin Hart and Dwayne Johnson.
You say *yuck* as if he said Liam Neeson.

"Oh, so you're a *critic* now?"
See, he's forgotten another thing.
"Alphabetical," you remind him.

Their car drives off. Family rule: you watch until they get past the four-way stop that no one stops at. Your arm is numb. You can feel the baby (this is what you call her) wedged between your elbow and ribs like a Manila folder. Both of you know that you're holding her wrong; but she does you a favor and ignores it. The car passes the intersection. They honk twice: safe! Your sister's hand sticks out the sunroof, waves a backwards goodbye. Your brother-in-law has both hands on the wheel. This is his saving grace.

Goofy is on TV. He's different than you remember him. Less flat. Talks the same though. You can make your niece laugh by doing the voice: *Gawrsh. Ah-hyuck hyuck.* There's a YouTube video of a linguistics professor teaching a voice actor how to do it. Only three hundred views. Most of them coming from you in October. You were Goofy three Halloweens in a row. Would have been four but your curly hair got too big for the hat and your self-confidence too small for the shoes. You took them both to Goodwill. The hat didn't even make it inside. Volunteer gave you five for it right there. You gave the five to a beggar outside of Del Taco. His sign made you laugh: *Give me money or I'll vote for Trump.* The shoes, however, are still on the top shelf two years later. You try not to take it too personally. Sometimes you'll go into the store and pick them up, turn them over in your hand like you're cooking a pig over a flame, give them a real good spin. You'll check the size and then act heartbroken. Sometimes this will attract a potential buyer. But they never give the shoes a fair shot. They tug on the laces, lift the shoes up and down to test the weight, and maybe they even hold one up to their foot. But never do they try them on. You think about this more than you should. What's wrong with you that your old shoes won't sell? You decide it's the price. $3.50 is too cheap. Can't trust a shoe cheaper than apple juice. Call them. Leave a voicemail. Say just that. The thing about the apple juice.

You used a similar logic when your book didn't sell. Just the same, you blamed it on the price. Only $13.99 for a hardback? "For fuck's sake, Franny!" is what you said when the first month's sales came in. You heard Grandpa say that to Grandma when you were a kid. You loved the rhythm of the words. You loved how the alliteration stampeded through the house, anger Trojan-horsed as poetry. So when it was finally your chance to yell it, you didn't edit out the *Franny* — even though the only other person in the room that day was named Stuart.

(The rest of the Goofy costume is still in your closet. You wear the orange sweater in November. Feels like you're a pumpkin. You wear the pants to nice dinners. Feels like you're getting away with something.)

Your niece is trying to climb up the ottoman, her small body blocking the big TV. When her hand slips, she falls and cries. You're not allowed to help her. (Her rule, not yours.) She's going through that independent phase. Doesn't want your help but still needs you for 99% of all human activities. When she gets to the top, she cries for you to get her down. And when you try to help her down, she cries for you to let her go. This back and forth goes on for a good while. You can't help but think of that scene from *The Notebook* of Gosling yelling *What Do You Want!* You act it out for the sake of comedy, forehead vein and all. Makes her cry even more. But it gives you a quick laugh. You get plenty of those since you stopped writing. You're at nine just today. You suspect by sundown you'll get to turn your hand at an angle and cross through four lines with a fifth. Tally marks — this is the purpose of your pens now. Ha. Pens. Remember the joke you said? You said it on an interview in your head. (Your body was driving the 405 up to LA, and your brain was on Oprah.) She asked you, "What would you have if you didn't have writing?" And you said, "Too many pens." The crowd laughed. And then Oprah told them to check under their seats where everyone found a signed copy of your book. They cheered as if they were actually going to read it.

Now when you daydream of being on Oprah, you're in the audience. Her guest is a man from Wisconsin who doesn't have sex with his wife because he's just too tired. Oprah brings up a sex counselor who tries to find a deeper, more interesting reason why the man is distant from his wife sexually. But in the end, after all the psychoanalysis, she concludes that the man is, indeed, *just too tired.*

You play this clip in your head and laugh. You pull out a pen, whichever one you'd like, black, blue, or red. The color no longer means anything. You use the baby's back as your clipboard, and you give yourself a tally. Too many pens? Look at you now, making new use of old materials.

You go back to the couch and watch what part of Goofy you can see behind your niece on the ottoman: mostly shoes, a bit of the hat.

When it's just you and the baby it's like the house is empty, and an empty house isn't good for you. It never has been. Remember when Mom used to go to the grocery store? You'd beg her not to go. You'd tell her that being out of jelly isn't such a bad thing. Peanut butter pairs better with banana anyway. When she left, you'd log on to the family computer and you'd look up images of famous women in bathing suits: Eva Longoria yellow bathing suit, Paris Hilton yellow bathing suit, Jessica Alba yellow bathing suit. You copy and pasted the images to Microsoft Paint. From there you could see all three images at once. No scrolling or anything. A porn prodigy, you thought of yourself. What a tragic talent to discover as a preteen. Most of your talents are tragedies, the writing and the thinking especially.

When Mom came home, you'd leave the image searches open on purpose; and she'd send you to your room — where you were free to sit in silence without her worrying about your preferred solitude. You did some of your best writing and thinking up there in timeout.

An empty house does different things to you now at twenty-six. There used to be so many impulses, the women in yellow bathing suits, the soda in the fridge, the matches in the drawer third from the bottom. Now there's just one. But it's stronger than any other that's ever taken you over. You pick up the book you wrote three years ago. (It's not kept on a bookshelf. The baby uses it as a toy. The family uses it as a coaster.)

And you place a different book inside of it: Peter Orner's *Last Car Over The Sagamore Bridge*. You read out loud. Your voice fills the house, the perfectly written words of an author you envy come out of your mouth as if they are your very own; and you imagine they are your very own. You get in such a rhythm you truly believe they are yours; you would swear on it. Hand on the Bible or the heart, doesn't matter. The words are yours. And they are perfect. It's a pleasure like no other.

You go on and on. You don't stop. A slight pause for punctuation, but the next word is never too far away.

There's a scratch in your throat but you know better than to cough. Reminds baby of Dad. Your mouth is dry but you know better than to use the sink. Reminds her of Mom. The trick to babysitting (and isn't this sad?) is to convince the baby their parents don't exist. When your sister and brother-in-law come home, you'll have to put the family photos back on the wall. You've stacked them in the closet. Even put a blanket over the exercise bike. You're full of tricks. Fifteen-dollars-an-hour type of tricks. Although, five goes to the nine-year-old neighbor who comes over to change the diaper for you. Another trick of yours. It's a good system. If you feed her mostly bread you can keep your wallet in your pocket.

This neighbor's quite the entrepreneur though. Calls you on the hour. Partly for the payday, and partly so she can hear you tell stories while she changes the diaper. She wants to have stories like you one day. That's what she's told you. Squeezed your hand tight and promised you one day she'll tell you the greatest story you've ever heard.

She's a story herself, doesn't even know it yet. Wears her Grandma's old Converse. Peeled off the star and stitched her initials on instead. Won't tell you how to spell her name. It could be Y or it could be with an I. Doesn't matter, she said. Said she tested that philosophy in a spelling bee. Placed last: hidrogen.

You turn the last page. You are out of words and out of breath. You clear your throat and get some water. The baby cries for Mom and Dad.

It's 7 p.m. Take out your phone, answer it on the first ring. No hellos on either end. It's business off the bat.

You say to your neighbor, "Nothin'." She says, "Sniff the butt." Instead you use a wafting technique. It's not an accurate measure, but it's more your style. You stand behind your niece, who's laughing at a Hot Wheels commercial, and you sniff into the phone to make your effort heard.

"Nothin'," you tell her. "No," she says. "Sniff the butt!" Set the phone down, put it on speaker, pick up the baby and bring her diaper toward your face. She cries. You laugh. She smells like a petting zoo. You react accordingly, with coughs, two curse words, and then more laughter as you look toward a five sticking out of your wallet across the room.

Hot Wheels are gone. Goofy is back. He's the only one laughing. The baby is screaming. The neighbor is bartering.

"Sounds like a ten," she says over the phone.

"Smells like a twenty," you warn her, *"Ah-hyuck hyuck!"*

The neighbor does the diaper. It's like a slide puzzle to you. It's like a science to her. "Story," is all she says. You have hundreds in your head. They are perfect up there. You've promised never to bring these ones to paper. That's where they start to haunt you.

You tell her the one about the sixty-three-year-old man who rents a room in a young woman's apartment for five hundred dollars — four hundred and eighty before the young woman double checks his counting. This old man only talks in numbers. *Five hundred* when he hands her the rent. *Seven* when he wants her to change the channel. *Four twenty-five* when he sees her contemplating the oven and a sweet potato. One day she tries to get the man to say real words. She asks, "How was your Grandson's soccer game?" He says his first complete sentence: "They won." But still, she only hears a number.

You tell her the one about the French cousin who comes to town, how the American girl prepares for his arrival by salting all the snails in Grandma's courtyard in case he's hungry from the long flight. He is older, smoking a cigarette, and declines the snails offered to him atop a dirty palm. The American girl says something like, "But don't the French eat snails?" He'd hate for her to be embarrassed, so he says something like, "Yes, but I'm on diet." The French cousin says not to worry, the dead snails won't go to waste; and he holds her free hand all the way to the park, where they feed snails to the ducks.

At school on Monday, the American girl has to present to the class what she learned over the weekend. She stands on top of her desk and says, "Ducks are French," and then she sits back down.

You tell her about the father who writes reminders to himself before heading to bed. He hunches over a yellow flash card and writes in big, blocky letters with a black marker — staying up an extra minute past his preferred bedtime to take care of his future self, to give some guidance to the tired old man who leaves for work at four thirty in the morning. *Don't forget your lunch. Meeting at 3:15.* Things like that. When he finally retires, he has to write a note that night. He zombie walks halfway down the stairs the next morning and sees it on the front door: *Go back to bed, Jack. It's finally over.* In bed that morning, his wife jokes, pretending to be doing long division on her pillow, that if he didn't spend so much money on yellow flashcards, tape, and black markers, he would have been able to retire fifteen years ago.

You tell her about the mother who pays her son five dollars to tell her jokes at open mics because she's scared to tell them herself: "Is me accidently biting my tongue the equivalent of a Deaf person hitting their funny bone?"

You tell her the one about the suicidal husband in the red sweater at church. He's worse at praying than he is drinking, but it's Sunday and he'll have to kiss his wife on the lips; and she can't smell god nearly as well as vodka. He changes out of his sweater before going back home. Tells his wife he was playing tennis. No one expects anything is wrong with a man who plays tennis. He goes straight to the shower to sell it. "Sweating pretty good," he murmurs.

"One more," she asks, no longer doing anything productive with the diaper, just picking at the fuzz and handing it to the baby to play with. "But do it how you do it in the books. With everything coming together just right."

You tell her that you don't write books anymore. That they hurt too much.

The diaper has no more fuzz to pick. The baby is asleep on the ground. Is this allowed? You aren't sure. The neighbor brings you your book and says, "Read it."

You hold your book without another book hiding inside. And still, it feels heavier than it should. You look at the pages for the first time since you toured it.

"Read it."

She lays with you on the couch and rests the back of her head on your lap. She kicks off her shoes. Tells you that she's not used to laying this way, face up. You don't understand. Spankings, she says. Tells you that her Mom doesn't know where she is. Tells you that the idea of her Dad makes her smile, but the man himself makes her cry. That her Mom's favorite word is cunt. That she's allowed to say it, too. That her Dad speaks with his hands. Sometimes a fist. That stories in books are better than real life. Read it, she says again.

You close the book. And then your eyes. And you say this, slowly, carefully, as if you can't afford to get it wrong, as if someone's life depends on this paragraph, as if you were at your desk writing again, trying to make the world laugh, guiding their eyes left to right, putting your own well-being aside, and there's a feeling that the words have been waiting, and so you say them, slowly, but without pause:

She wears her Grandma's old Converse. Peeled off the star and stitched her initials on instead. Won't tell you how to spell her name. It could be Y or it could be with an I. Doesn't matter, she said. Said she tested that philosophy in a spelling bee. Placed last: hidrogen.

There are pens in your pocket. They never left. Choose one. The right one. The one for starting something new. Now start with this paragraph. Put it at the bottom and work backwards from here. Don't let it haunt you. Just write one word and then the next. After some time, you'll be at the title. Make it something funny. Make it give you something to smile about. And what's more important, make it something about your neighbor, that sweet girl. Because by the time you write your way up to the title, you'll have learned something that every author has learned, that these stories, once they are done, aren't yours any longer. So let them go. Don't let them haunt you. Go ahead. Highlight this document. Every word. Slide your fingers. Top to bottom. See all that blue.

Don't even think.

Now do it. Hit delete.

A Special Thanks

To D.J Harris (@djs_doodles) for making our drawings not suck. If it weren't for you, this book would have a lot more stick figures.

To our management team, Bx2 Entertainment. You believed in this weird project from Day One; and you helped us believe in it, too. You were there from first draft (yikes) to final print (yay). You kept us from putting our pages on a pedestal and you kept us from throwing the book in the trash bin. You talked us through our first time on a roller-coaster. We'll let you rest your voice for a minute. Grab some water. Get a churro. But be ready, we're already back in line.

To Claudia Sloan of Tallfellow Press for guiding us through this process with patience and passion; thank you for lending us your creativity and experience, and an even bigger thank you for caring about this book just as much as we do. And an additional thank you for introducing us to Roger Price's Droodles. *Bowling Ball For Man Who Likes To Make Decisions* will always make us laugh – and reliable laughter is invaluable when in the trenches of writing a book.

To Austin Cairo (sorry if we spelled your last name wrong but you haven't texted us back yet) for hearing our vision of an ideal book cover and then bringing those ideas to life. Let's howl at the moon sometime soon my brother.

To Jean Hwang for designing this wonderful cover and dealing with our mess of requests, our sloppy handwriting, our strange spacing and formatting habits, and our inability to operate a scanner.

To Janna Wong for proofreading. Knowing we had someone to clean up our inadequacies saved us a lot of worry. The *was* vs. *were* debate when dealing with improbable, conditional clauses when the subject of the sentence is third person singular was often resolved by a coin flip and the understanding that we'd have a proofreader there to change heads to tails if need be.

To the coffee shops and bars that gave us a place to write all day and all night. If we make just five dollars on this book, it's going in your tip jar.

To the people who read books. Without you, we'd be the crazy men on the street yelling at cars. Thank you for pulling over and rolling down the windows for us.

To our families for understanding that we wanted to use our dedication page as an opportunity to make a joke rather than dedicate the book to them. We love you.

About the Authors

Photo by Tien Nguyen

Darren Nuzzo (@darrennuzzo) is a writer and performer from Southern California. His fiction has been anthologized in literary journals and his birthday cards to Mom have made it to the fridge. Darren built a cult social media following through his lengthy literary captions on Instagram. As a fitness guru, sustainability advocate, self-proclaimed wizard, and hippie at heart, Darren brings a unique outlook to his writing.

Toddy Smith (@todderic_) is a performer, writer and leading digital content creator (and member of the Vlog Squad) who has amassed a following of over 4 million adoring fans. Toddy uses his eccentric storytelling to share a glimpse into his and his friends' lives through vlogs and other comedic content across his social channels. He lives in Southern California where he is most often found at his piano.